LIVING  LITURGY™

for Extraordinary Ministers of Holy Communion

Year A • 2020

Brian Schmisek
Katy Beedle Rice
Diana Macalintal

LITURGICAL PRESS
Collegeville, Minnesota

www.litpress.org

Cover design by Monica Bokinskie. Art by Ned Bustard (pages 6–14, 58–62, 96–122), Emanuel Franco-Gómez, OCarm (cover and pages 16–24, 38–54, 86–94), and Tanja Butler (pages 26–36, 64–84, 124–40).

ISSN 1933-3129

ISBN 978-0-8146-4424-9   ISBN 978-0-8146-4449-2 (ebook)

Presented to

_____

in grateful appreciation
for ministering as an
Extraordinary Minister
of
Holy Communion

_____

_____

(date)

USING THIS RESOURCE

Extraordinary typically refers to outstanding or exceptional.
But extraordinary ministers of Holy Communion are "extra"-
ordinary in the sense of "in addition to" the ordinary (as well as
being outstanding and exceptional!). Ordinary ministers of Holy
Communion are the ordained and those properly installed as
acolytes, usually seminarians. In parishes today there are simply
not enough "ordinary" ministers of Holy Communion, so we call
forth additional ministers, referred to as "extraordinary." Imagine
how long the distribution of Communion would take if only the
ordained or seminarians were those who distributed! It is not only
because of need, however, that we have extraordinary ministers
of Holy Communion. It is also by virtue of one's baptism. We
parishioners are grateful that so many baptized Christians respond to the call to serve as extraordinary ministers of Holy Communion. In so doing we are reminded that we are all holy, and we
are all called to ministry by virtue of our Christian baptism.

Preparing for This Ministry

Though different dioceses and parishes have slightly different
preparation requirements for those who would be extraordinary
ministers of Holy Communion, there is preparation nonetheless.
We hope that this book will be a source of reflection for such
preparation, and also for ongoing reflection throughout one's ministry. We know that it is not enough to simply attend a training
event and never look back. Each ministry of the church requires
regular prayer, reflection, reading, and thoughtfulness. This book
is intended to assist with that process by providing prayers and
reflection for each Sunday and for certain solemnities. This resource can also be used by groups who would like to share their
faith with questions that prompt discussion.

Holy Communion for the Homebound and Sick

In the New Testament Letter of James we learn about the concern
and care that the early Christians had for those members of their
community who were sick. Such care and concern was a hallmark
of Jesus' own ministry, and it has been a Christian charism ever
since. Each week there are parishioners who are not able to join us

for the liturgy, and so the Eucharist is brought to them as a sign of our unity. Extraordinary ministers of Holy Communion are often those who perform this ministry, and, in so doing, they extend the parish's reach to so many more fellow parishioners. This book is intended to be a resource for them as well.

Adapting This Resource for Holy Communion for the Homebound and Sick
The Communion rite (Ordinary Rite of Communion of the Sick) is provided as a separate publication to this book and enclosed within. Those who are extraordinary ministers of Holy Communion have undoubtedly been made familiar with this rite as part of their preparation. This book may be adapted for use with the rite, by sharing the gospel reflection, the prayers, or even the reflection question, so that the visit becomes a true ministry. It is to be remembered that ministers are not mere functionaries. As such, extraordinary ministers of Holy Communion bring not only the presence of Christ in the eucharistic species, but the presence of Christ in their very person by virtue of their baptism. So this book has been designed with that in mind, and it can be used to assist with making this a meaningful encounter and ministry.

On this First Sunday of Advent we come before the Lord with hopeful hearts and joyful spirits, and ask him to once again send his light to illuminate the darkness in our lives . . .

Prayer

God of new beginnings,
we give thanks that we may stand within your gates
and rejoice in your holy temple.
May your peace dwell with us always.
Show us, Lord, your love,
and grant us your salvation. **Amen.**

Gospel   **Matt 24:37-44**

Jesus said to his disciples: "As it was in the days of Noah, so it will be at the coming of the Son of Man. In those days before the flood, they were eating and drinking, marrying and giving in marriage, up to the day that Noah entered the ark. They did not know until the flood came and carried them all away. So will it be also at the coming of the Son of Man. Two men will be out in the field; one will be taken, and one will be left. Two women will be grinding at the mill; one will be taken, and one will be left. Therefore, stay awake! For you do not know on which day your Lord will come. Be sure of this: if the master of the house had known the hour of night when the thief was coming, he would have stayed awake and not let his house be broken into. So too, you also must be prepared, for at an hour you do not expect, the Son of Man will come."

Brief Silence

For Reflection

"Stay awake!" These words in the Gospel of Matthew today strike us to the core as we begin the Advent season. These words also foreshadow the disciples' struggle during the agony in the garden. The call to stay awake presumes that we might be dozing off, idling our time away. Disciples must be ready at all times without resorting to a false sense of security.

Jesus tells his audience that as it was in the time of Noah, so shall it be at the coming of the Lord. In Noah's day, human beings went steadily on their way, unaware and apparently unconcerned that something larger was at work. Yet, "the flood came and carried them all away." Jesus tells his listeners that the Son of Man will come when we do not expect it. These words were written for Matthew's community, which might have grown complacent during the intervening decades between Jesus' time on earth and the composition of the gospel. But these same words are for us, even two thousand years later. Rather than expecting a cataclysmic event like the flood of Noah or something apocalyptic, we might consider our own death, which may come when we least expect it.

✦ In the gospel Jesus urges the disciples to "stay awake! / For you do not know on which day your Lord will come." What is Jesus calling you to "wake up" to this Advent?

Brief Silence

Prayer

Lord God, you sent your Son as light for the world. May we be watchful for that same light as we anticipate his coming, mindful of the signs that he is near. Let us not grow weary but instead be ever vigilant. We ask this in his name, for he is the dawn that breaks from on high. **Amen.**

In today's gospel John the Baptist tells us, "Repent, for the kingdom of heaven is at hand!" For the times we have not lived lives worthy of God's kingdom of justice and peace, let us ask for forgiveness . . .

Prayer

God of all nations, you chose John the Baptist
to be your voice in the desert.
May our voices join with his to announce that your salvation is near.
Justice shall flourish in his time,
and fullness of peace forever. **Amen.**

Gospel   **Matt 3:1-12**

John the Baptist appeared, preaching in the desert of Judea and saying, "Repent, for the kingdom of heaven is at hand!" It was of him that the prophet Isaiah had spoken when he said: / *A voice of one crying out in the desert, / Prepare the way of the Lord, / make straight his paths.* / John wore clothing made of camel's hair and had a leather belt around his waist. His food was locusts and wild honey. At that time Jerusalem, all Judea, and the whole region around the Jordan were going out to him and were being baptized by him in the Jordan River as they acknowledged their sins.

When he saw many of the Pharisees and Sadducees coming to his baptism, he said to them, "You brood of vipers! Who warned you to flee from the coming wrath? Produce good fruit as evidence of your repentance. And do not presume to say to yourselves, 'We have Abraham as our father.' For I tell you, God can raise up children to Abraham from these stones. Even now the ax lies at the root of the trees. Therefore every tree that does not bear good fruit will be cut down and thrown into the fire. I am baptizing you with water, for repentance, but the one who is coming after me is mightier than I. I am not worthy to carry his sandals. He will baptize you with the Holy Spirit and fire. His winnowing fan is in his hand. He will clear his threshing floor and gather his wheat into his barn, but the chaff he will burn with unquenchable fire."

Brief Silence

For Reflection

Though today is December 8 when we might expect the solemnity of the Immaculate Conception, it happens to fall on a Sunday. Therefore, the Second Sunday of Advent is what we celebrate today. We will commemorate the Immaculate Conception tomorrow. And for this Advent Sunday we hear the fiery preaching of John the Baptist, introduced for the first time in the Gospel of Matthew.

Because John the Baptist is considered a Christian saint, it's sometimes possible to overlook that historically he was a Jewish prophet calling the Jewish people to repentance, as prophets had done for centuries before. He directly confronts the Pharisees and Sadducees, name-calling them a "brood of vipers." They are not to rest assured in their being part of the chosen people of God, the children of Abraham. For God can raise up children of Abraham from the stones. This message is so stark it nearly needs to be recast to our own day for those of us who might feel secure in our Christian or Catholic identity. We can hear John telling us that God can make Christians from the stones. There is no inherent value or guarantee of salvation simply by being Christian. John would say something more is demanded. We are to repent, for the kingdom is at hand.

✦ John the Baptist tells us, "Repent, for the kingdom of heaven is at hand!" Rather than rest secure in our Christian identity, from what do we need to repent?

Brief Silence

Prayer

Lord God Almighty, you sent John the Baptist to call your people to repentance. May we heed that same message, speaking to us through the ages. Grant us the courage to turn away from all that keeps us from you, so that we may embrace the Kingdom of Heaven. **Amen.**

THE IMMACULATE CONCEPTION OF THE BLESSED VIRGIN MARY

On this feast of the Immaculate Conception, we ponder Mary's proclamation: "May it be done to me according to your word." Let us ask for healing for the times our own faith in God's goodness has wavered . . .

Prayer

Prepared from birth to trust in you,
Mary believed in your Word, O God.
May we share her faith that all things are possible with you.
Sing to the Lord a new song,
for God has done marvelous deeds. **Amen.**

Gospel   **Luke 1:26-38**

The angel Gabriel was sent from God to a town of Galilee called Nazareth, to a virgin betrothed to a man named Joseph, of the house of David, and the virgin's name was Mary. And coming to her, he said, "Hail, full of grace! The Lord is with you." But she was greatly troubled at what was said and pondered what sort of greeting this might be. Then the angel said to her, "Do not be afraid, Mary, for you have found favor with God. Behold, you will conceive in your womb and bear a son, and you shall name him Jesus. He will be great and will be called Son of the Most High, and the Lord God will give him the throne of David his father, and he will rule over the house of Jacob forever, and of his Kingdom there will be no end." But Mary said to the angel, "How can this be, since I have no relations with a man?" And the angel said to her in reply, "The Holy Spirit will come upon you, and the power of the Most High will overshadow you. Therefore the child to be born will be called holy, the Son of God. And behold, Elizabeth, your relative, has also conceived a son in her old age, and this is the sixth month for her who was called barren; for nothing will be impossible for God." Mary said, "Behold, I am the handmaid of the Lord. May it be done to me according to your word." Then the angel departed from her.

Brief Silence

For Reflection

In movies and TV series, the angel of the annunciation is depicted in a variety of ways, sometimes as a light from offscreen (as in Franco Zeffirelli's *Jesus of Nazareth* [1977]) or other times in a more graphic way much as a human being (as in *The Nativity Story* [2006]). But Luke does not describe the angel Gabriel. The reader is left to fill in the details. We do not even know what time of day it was. And other than Nazareth, a small Galilean village, we don't know where Mary was when this happened. Was this at home? On the road? In a field? Luke does not tell us. So it is interesting to ask ourselves how many details we have naturally filled in after hearing the story. The way we fill in these details conveys much about our own theological perspectives. Luke is content to say the angel Gabriel was sent from God to Nazareth. The subsequent conversation between Gabriel and Mary set the course of human history.

This gospel reading is proclaimed when we celebrate today the Immaculate Conception, the purity of Mary from the moment she herself was conceived. These theological mysteries are worthy of reflection, thought, prayer, and conversation with other Christians.

✦ As the model disciple, Mary shows us the way to live a life completely devoted to Christ. How would you like to emulate Mary more fully in this coming year?

Brief Silence

Prayer

Good and gracious God, the way of your Son was prepared by Mary, his mother. May her model of discipleship inspire us to be open to your will. Grant us a heart like her own, devoted to you above all else. We ask this in the name of her son. **Amen.**

In today's gospel John's disciples ask Jesus, "Are you the one who is to come, / or should we look for another?" For the times we have looked elsewhere instead of focusing our gaze on Christ, let us ask for mercy and pardon . . .

Prayer

The signs of your glory, O God, are all around us
in the blind who see, the deaf who hear, and the dead raised to
    new life.
May our song announce glad tidings to all in need.
The Lord shall reign forever,
the Lord who comes to save us. **Amen.**

Gospel   **Matt 11:2-11**

When John the Baptist heard in prison of the works of the Christ, he sent his disciples to Jesus with this question, "Are you the one who is to come, or should we look for another?" Jesus said to them in reply, "Go and tell John what you hear and see: the blind regain their sight, the lame walk, lepers are cleansed, the deaf hear, the dead are raised, and the poor have the good news proclaimed to them. And blessed is the one who takes no offense at me."

As they were going off, Jesus began to speak to the crowds about John, "What did you go out to the desert to see? A reed swayed by the wind? Then what did you go out to see? Someone dressed in fine clothing? Those who wear fine clothing are in royal palaces. Then why did you go out? To see a prophet? Yes, I tell you, and more than a prophet. This is the one about whom it is written: / *Behold, I am sending my messenger ahead of you; / he will prepare your way before you.* / Amen, I say to you, among those born of women there has been none greater than John the Baptist; yet the least in the kingdom of heaven is greater than he."

Brief Silence

For Reflection

John the Baptist's presence features prominently in the gospel today. Though we are in the midst of Jesus' ministry and John is in prison, he has a question for the would-be Christ: "Are you the one who is to come / or should we look for another?" Though it might be surprising to us, it seems as though Jesus did not fit the expectations of John the Baptist! Two thousand years later, we see these figures through the eyes of faith and so it can be difficult to place ourselves in the context of their day.

John the Baptist had been preaching fiery judgment, imminent wrath. Last week's gospel itself states this message quite plainly. In John's mind, the one to come would baptize with the Holy Spirit and with fire. The winnowing fan is in his hand. The chaff will be burned in an unquenchable fire. But then John is arrested and imprisoned, and Jesus begins preaching and doing mighty deeds. There is not the judgment that John expected. Thus, he sends his own disciples from his imprisonment with an astonishing question for Jesus. Had John gotten it wrong? Is Jesus the one? Or is there another? Jesus' mission is not exactly what John had in mind. Jesus is proclaiming and initiating the kingdom of God.

✦ The disciples of John the Baptist ask Jesus, "Are you the one who is to come, / or should we look for another?" In our culture, what do you think are the greatest temptations that lead us to turn our gaze from Christ and to search for fulfillment elsewhere?

Brief Silence

Prayer

God of love, mercy, and repentance, you prepared the way of your Son by sending John the Baptist, whose own expectations were exceeded. Give us the openness of mind and thought to recognize your work in the world, even when that exceeds, or may be quite different from, our own expectations. We humbly pray. **Amen.**

In today's gospel the angel of the Lord tells Joseph, "[D]o not be afraid to take Mary your wife into your home." For the times fear has kept us from following God's will for our lives, let us turn to God for mercy . . .

Prayer

Your name, Emmanuel, is your promise that we are not alone.
Help us be more like Joseph that we may never fear
to open our homes and our hearts to your presence.
Let the Lord enter
for he is the king of glory. **Amen.**

Gospel   Matt 1:18-24

This is how the birth of Jesus Christ came about. When his mother Mary was betrothed to Joseph, but before they lived together, she was found with child through the Holy Spirit. Joseph her husband, since he was a righteous man, yet unwilling to expose her to shame, decided to divorce her quietly. Such was his intention when, behold, the angel of the Lord appeared to him in a dream and said, "Joseph, son of David, do not be afraid to take Mary your wife into your home. For it is through the Holy Spirit that this child has been conceived in her. She will bear a son and you are to name him Jesus, because he will save his people from their sins." All this took place to fulfill what the Lord had said through the prophet: / *Behold, the virgin shall conceive and bear a son, / and they shall name him Emmanuel,* / which means "God is with us." / When Joseph awoke, he did as the angel of the Lord had commanded him and took his wife into his home.

Brief Silence

For Reflection

On this Fourth Sunday of Advent we have a story about Joseph told by Matthew. There are so few stories where Joseph is even named in the New Testament that it is good to read this one carefully. We have no words from Joseph in this story or any other in the New Testament. He is a quiet but righteous man, doing what is right in the sight of God.

Thus, Joseph's desire to end the relationship with Mary quietly upon finding out that she is with child is in keeping with his character. But the appearance of an angel in Joseph's dream is enough to change his mind. He takes his wife into his home in Bethlehem (not Nazareth, as Luke has it). Later the child will be born there, at the home.

As for now, the stage is set for Christmas morning, the nativity of our Lord. A discreet, quiet man who does what is right in the sight of God has taken the pregnant Mary into his home as his wife. What was a scandal worthy of death under the law has been directed by an angel in a dream into safety and security for the woman and her unborn child. God is doing something new.

✦ In the gospel we hear the familiar phrase "[D]o not be afraid." Where do you see fear affecting your family, community, or society at large?

Brief Silence

Prayer

Lord Jesus Christ, your coming brings peace to the world. Make us instruments of that same peace, for when we are known as peacemakers, we will be known as your own. We ask this in your name, the Prince of Peace. **Amen.**

As we prepare to enter into the mystery of the incarnation, God become human to dwell among us, let us pause and offer to God our very selves, our triumphs as well as our failings, trusting in God's infinite mercy . . .

Prayer

Wonder-Counselor, you guide us in right paths:
Glory to God in the highest!
God-Hero, you fill us with hope:
Glory to God in the highest!
Father-Forever, you never abandon us:
Glory to God in the highest!
Prince of Peace, you dispel our darkness:
Glory to God in the highest! **Amen.**

Gospel   Luke 2:1-14 (Mass at Midnight)

In those days a decree went out from Caesar Augustus that the whole world should be enrolled. This was the first enrollment, when Quirinius was governor of Syria. So all went to be enrolled, each to his own town. And Joseph too went up from Galilee from the town of Nazareth to Judea, to the city of David that is called Bethlehem, because he was of the house and family of David, to be enrolled with Mary, his betrothed, who was with child. While they were there, the time came for her to have her child, and she gave birth to her firstborn son. She wrapped him in swaddling clothes and laid him in a manger, because there was no room for them in the inn.

Now there were shepherds in that region living in the fields and keeping the night watch over their flock. The angel of the Lord appeared to them and the glory of the Lord shone around them, and they were struck with great fear. The angel said to them, "Do not be afraid; for behold, I proclaim to you good news of great joy that will be for all the people. For today in the city of David a savior has been born for you who is Christ and Lord. And this will be a sign for you: you will find an infant wrapped in swaddling clothes and lying in a manger." And suddenly there was a multitude of the heavenly host with the angel, praising God and saying: / "Glory to God in the highest / and on earth peace to those on whom his favor rests."

Brief Silence

For Reflection

The reading from Luke at the Midnight Mass is both sublime and popular. Even the 1965 Peanuts Christmas special, *A Charlie Brown Christmas,* features this gospel passage, read by the character Linus. The master storyteller Luke enraptures us with the story of Jesus' birth. The simple clause "because there was no room for them at the inn" has inspired innumerable artists, homilists, theologians, and more. But Luke says no more about that episode than those few simple words. He says much more about the shepherds, the angel, and the multitude of the heavenly host. The few verses of this gospel reading light up our imagination, touching on key themes for Luke, such as Jesus as Savior, Jesus as food for the world (laid him in a *manger*), and the situation of the Christ-event at a particular time and place (with mention of Quirinius and the town of Bethlehem). How appropriate that we read this story of the shepherds keeping the night watch at our Midnight Mass. We recall how God brings life from death, joy from sadness, and light from darkness.

✦ When have you encountered God bringing life from death, joy from sadness, and light from darkness, in your own life?

Brief Silence

Prayer

Lord Jesus Christ, Savior of the world. Your birth was accompanied by angels singing Glory to God. May that joy animate us too as we witness you in our world, when we see light shining in the darkness, when we see hope in place of despair. We ask this in your name. **Amen.**

THE HOLY FAMILY OF JESUS, MARY, AND JOSEPH

In the Holy Family we find a model of love, service, and unity. Let us pause to ask Mary, Joseph, and Jesus to intercede for us for the times we have failed to imitate them . . .

Prayer

With a father's love and a mother's care,
you have made us your children, O God.
Make our families holy not by perfection but by love.
May the peace of Christ be in our hearts.
May the word of Christ dwell in us richly. **Amen.**

Gospel   **Matt 2:13-15, 19-23**

When the magi had departed, behold, the angel of the Lord appeared to Joseph in a dream and said, "Rise, take the child and his mother, flee to Egypt, and stay there until I tell you. Herod is going to search for the child to destroy him." Joseph rose and took the child and his mother by night and departed for Egypt. He stayed there until the death of Herod, that what the Lord had said through the prophet might be fulfilled, *Out of Egypt I called my son.*

When Herod had died, behold, the angel of the Lord appeared in a dream to Joseph in Egypt and said, "Rise, take the child and his mother and go to the land of Israel, for those who sought the child's life are dead." He rose, took the child and his mother, and went to the land of Israel. But when he heard that Archelaus was ruling over Judea in place of his father Herod, he was afraid to go back there. And because he had been warned in a dream, he departed for the region of Galilee. He went and dwelt in a town called Nazareth, so that what had been spoken through the prophets might be fulfilled, *He shall be called a Nazorean.*

Brief Silence

For Reflection

It's likely that in our own minds we've conflated the nativity stories of Luke and Matthew into one. But reading Matthew on his own terms reveals something fascinating. In Matthew's telling, Joseph and Mary had a home in Bethlehem, where Jesus was born. The magi eventually found their way to the home to find the *child* Jesus (not the infant). And now Joseph takes the *child* and his mother into Egypt. Only after Herod had died did Joseph have the courage to return. Even then, he was inspired by an angel in a dream! And he did not return to Bethlehem, but instead made his way to Nazareth.

In our modern world, we are witnessing a magnitude of migration of peoples not seen since World War II. As Christians, how do we treat these people? Can we see the Holy Family in their plight? It can be one thing to look with pity on the Holy Family and their flight into Egypt. But what of the lived reality of this biblical story in the lives of so many in our world today? May we as followers of this child refugee, this migrant Holy Family, recognize that same presence today and, in so doing, act on their behalf.

✦ In the gospel reading today Mary, Joseph, and Jesus face extreme peril. What has been the most difficult experience you have encountered as a member of your family? What helped you make it through this time?

Brief Silence

Prayer

Jesus Christ, Son of God and son of Mary, you were born into a family. By this birth you show us the holiness of family life with its struggles, joys, daily tasks, and bonds of love. Strengthen the relationships we have with our families as they are a source of holiness and spirituality for us. In your name we pray. **Amen.**

We gather on this solemnity of Mary, holy Mother of God, to listen to the words of Scripture and to be fed at the table of the Lord. Let us prepare our hearts and minds by recalling the places in our lives where we require God's healing and mercy . . .

Prayer

At the dawn of this New Year of grace, O Lord,
help us be present each day, like Mary,
to the blessings you have prepared for your people.
May God bless us in his mercy;
may the nations be glad and exult. **Amen.**

Gospel   **Luke 2:16-21**

The shepherds went in haste to Bethlehem and found Mary and Joseph, and the infant lying in the manger. When they saw this, they made known the message that had been told them about this child. All who heard it were amazed by what had been told them by the shepherds. And Mary kept all these things, reflecting on them in her heart. Then the shepherds returned, glorifying and praising God for all they had heard and seen, just as it had been told to them.

When eight days were completed for his circumcision, he was named Jesus, the name given him by the angel before he was conceived in the womb.

Brief Silence

For Reflection

We begin the secular New Year with the solemnity of Mary, the Mother of God. Mary's role in the life of Jesus was paramount, as is the role of any mother in a child's life, even in absence. We can imagine the lessons Jesus learned from his mother, who was chosen by God for this relationship. In the same Gospel of Luke from which we read today, we learn that Mary has a heart for the poor, the downtrodden, and the neglected when we hear her *Magnificat*. This was the spirit that animated her before Jesus was born; we can imagine it animated and influenced him too.

When we consider Jesus' role and identity through the lens of Mary, we often gain a new insight into his personhood. We know from Luke that Mary was present at many of the events in Jesus' life—and even after his earthly life when she was present with the disciples.

Today, let us renew our appreciation for Mary and her role in the life of Jesus, and by extension may we renew our appreciation for all mothers and the role they play in the life of their children.

✦ Mary not only physically carries the Word of God within her womb and brings it to birth, she continues to nurture this Word her whole life long. How might we follow Mary's example of nurturing?

Brief Silence

Prayer

God Almighty, Lord of heaven and earth, you sent your son into the world with Mary as his mother. May her spirit of attentiveness to the poor and outcast touch us in our day, so that we might, like her son, work for justice in the world, and thereby participate in the coming of the Kingdom of heaven. We ask this in the name of your Son, Jesus our Lord. **Amen.**

In the first reading, the prophet Isaiah proclaims, "Rise up in splendor, Jerusalem! Your light has come." On this feast of Epiphany let us greet Jesus Christ, the light of the world, and invite him to illuminate the darkness within our lives . . .

Prayer

Where darkness covers the earth, your glory, Lord, shines.
Where nations walk in fear, your star lights the way.
Help us always to follow where you lead.
All you lands, raise your eyes and see:
Our God has come to save us. **Amen.**

Gospel   **Matt 2:1-12**

When Jesus was born in Bethlehem of Judea, in the days of King Herod, behold, magi from the east arrived in Jerusalem, saying, "Where is the newborn king of the Jews? We saw his star at its rising and have come to do him homage." When King Herod heard this, he was greatly troubled, and all Jerusalem with him. Assembling all the chief priests and the scribes of the people, he inquired of them where the Christ was to be born. They said to him, "In Bethlehem of Judea, for thus it has been written through the prophet: / *And you, Bethlehem, land of Judah, / are by no means least among the rulers of Judah; / since from you shall come a ruler, / who is to shepherd my people Israel."* / Then Herod called the magi secretly and ascertained from them the time of the star's appearance. He sent them to Bethlehem and said, "Go and search diligently for the child. When you have found him, bring me word, that I too may go and do him homage." After their audience with the king they set out. And behold, the star that they had seen at its rising preceded them, until it came and stopped over the place where the child was. They were overjoyed at seeing the star, and on entering the house they saw the child with Mary his mother. They prostrated themselves and did him homage. Then they opened their treasures and offered him gifts of gold, frankincense, and myrrh. And having been warned in a dream not to return to Herod, they departed for their country by another way.

Brief Silence

For Reflection

This story of the magi gives us many points to consider. One might be the fact that Gentiles (considered "the other") come to worship Jesus. Herod needs to ask his advisors about the prophecy when those from Persia (Gentiles) are seeking out the child on their own. We, too, might be open to the other, those who come to the truth and to the person of Jesus on their own accord or by following their own stars. We know that by the end of the gospel, this is Jesus' intention too, that his teachings are not restricted to a few, but are open to all. This is the same gospel that will tell us that not everyone who says, "Lord, Lord" will enter the kingdom of heaven. Instead, entry is only for those who do the will of the Father. And the will of the Father is that we act mercifully, much like the magi of the gospel today.

Let us read the story carefully, with attention to detail. Matthew, the evangelist and theologian, has much to tell us about the great teacher and child-king Jesus.

✦ For the magi in today's gospel, nature itself, in the form of a star, proclaims the birth of Jesus, the Son of God. From your own encounters with the natural world, what have you gleaned about the God of creation?

Brief Silence

Prayer

Lord God of the universe, you make your presence known in the wonders of nature. Give us eyes to see your works in the world around us, so that we might be attentive to your creation in all its goodness. We ask this in the name of your son, through whom the world was made. **Amen.**

After Jesus' baptism in the Jordan River, a voice from the heavens proclaims, "This is my beloved Son, with whom I am well pleased." May this holy water remind us of the joy of our own baptism and strengthen us to live out our lives filled with the love of Jesus . . .

Prayer

Upon your Son, your favor rests, O God,
and through his baptism, you opened heaven to all who believe.
In Christ, may we be ever pleasing in your sight.
Give to the Lord glory and praise!
Glory to God in the highest! **Amen.**

Gospel   **Matt 3:13-17**

Jesus came from Galilee to John at the Jordan to be baptized by him. John tried to prevent him, saying, "I need to be baptized by you, and yet you are coming to me?" Jesus said to him in reply, "Allow it now, for thus it is fitting for us to fulfill all righteousness." Then he allowed him. After Jesus was baptized, he came up from the water and behold, the heavens were opened for him, and he saw the Spirit of God descending like a dove and coming upon him. And a voice came from the heavens, saying, "This is my beloved Son, with whom I am well pleased."

Brief Silence

For Reflection

Have you ever heard a story and then retold it to make it "better"? Maybe it was a question of timing, or introductions, or clarifying motivation. There are many ways stories are told and retold, and often they do get better in the retelling. This is what happens in today's gospel when we hear Matthew's version of the baptism of Jesus by John. The story Matthew had at hand was from Mark. There, John is said to have preached a baptism of repentance for the forgiveness of sins. So one question naturally arises: why would (sinless) Jesus undergo baptism for the forgiveness of sins? Also, Matthew has an entire infancy narrative with Joseph and Mary privy to his identity, something entirely absent from Mark's version. Thus, in Mark the heavenly voice says, "You are my beloved son" (addressed to Jesus). Not so in Matthew, where the heavenly voice says, "This is my beloved son." In Matthew, the voice is not for Jesus' sake but for the crowds. In these and in many other ways Matthew has improved the story—made it "better." Ultimately, the gospel passage is not so much about the baptism of Jesus as it is about the revelation of Jesus' identity to John and the others, including us.

✦ How is the revelation of Jesus' identity made known to you in our world today?

Brief Silence

Prayer

Lord Jesus, you were baptized in the Jordan, disclosing your identity as God's son. Give us the grace to recognize our identity as children of God by our own baptism. Secure in this identity, we will be your witnesses to the ends of the earth. In your name we pray. **Amen.**

In today's gospel, John the Baptist tells his disciples that Jesus is the Lamb of God who takes away the sins of the world. To prepare our hearts and minds to encounter Jesus in word and sacrament, let us offer up to him the burden of our own sins and ask for healing and mercy . . .

Prayer

Your Word, Lord, became flesh and dwelt among us
so that through his Spirit we may become your children.
May we always testify to his saving power.
You have put a new song in our mouths,
a hymn of praise to our gracious God. **Amen.**

Gospel   **John 1:29-34**

John the Baptist saw Jesus coming toward him and said, "Behold, the Lamb of God, who takes away the sin of the world. He is the one of whom I said, 'A man is coming after me who ranks ahead of me because he existed before me.' I did not know him, but the reason why I came baptizing with water was that he might be made known to Israel." John testified further, saying, "I saw the Spirit come down like a dove from heaven and remain upon him. I did not know him, but the one who sent me to baptize with water told me, 'On whomever you see the Spirit come down and remain, he is the one who will baptize with the Holy Spirit.' Now I have seen and testified that he is the Son of God."

Brief Silence

For Reflection

Most children love magicians, who sometimes say they are more properly called "illusionists." In reading today's gospel from John, we may think Jesus is baptized. But when we look at the story more carefully, we see that there's no baptism at all. John the Baptist's role is not to baptize Jesus. Instead, it is to testify to Jesus—a testament that, namely, Jesus is the Son of God. This title is significant for the Gospel of John, and it appears in the closing verse of the gospel (prior to the epilogue): "[T]hese [things] are written that you may come to believe that Jesus is the Christ, the Son of God, and that through this belief you may have life in his name" (20:31; NABRE).

So what John the Baptist testifies to in the beginning, that Jesus is the Son of God, is the entire purpose of the gospel. And all of this is done without Jesus being baptized. This gospel gracefully omits that detail. When we read the Gospel of John, let's pay special attention to the words he uses and the theological claims he makes. Otherwise, we might miss the essential truth and mistake it with a glance of an illusion.

✦ John the Baptist testifies to Jesus being the Son of God. What does that mean to you in your own life?

Brief Silence

Prayer

Lord Jesus, our brother and our Christ, you are son of God as testified to by John the Baptist. Give us, your modern-day disciples, the courage to testify to you in our own lives. By so doing we emulate the example of the Baptist and make you known throughout the world. In your name we pray. **Amen.**

In today's gospel Jesus calls two sets of brothers to join him in his work of proclaiming the kingdom of God. Immediately the brothers leave family and livelihood to follow him.

Let us ask for pardon and healing so that we, too, might follow the Lord of life with single-hearted love . . .

Prayer

Your Son, O God, fulfilled your promise
to bring light to all overshadowed by death.
May we dwell with Christ in your house all our days.
The Lord is my light and my salvation;
No one shall I fear. **Amen.**

Gospel   Matt 4:12-23 (or Matt 4:12-17)

When Jesus heard that John had been arrested, he withdrew to Galilee. He left Nazareth and went to live in Capernaum by the sea, in the region of Zebulun and Naphtali, that what had been said through Isaiah the prophet might be fulfilled: / *Land of Zebulun and land of Naphtali, / the way to the sea, beyond the Jordan, / Galilee of the Gentiles, / the people who sit in darkness have seen a great light, / on those dwelling in a land overshadowed by death / light has arisen.* / From that time on, Jesus began to preach and say, "Repent, for the kingdom of heaven is at hand."

As he was walking by the Sea of Galilee, he saw two brothers, Simon who is called Peter, and his brother Andrew, casting a net into the sea; they were fishermen. He said to them, "Come after me, and I will make you fishers of men." At once they left their nets and followed him. He walked along from there and saw two other brothers, James, the son of Zebedee, and his brother John.

They were in a boat, with their father Zebedee, mending their nets. He called them, and immediately they left their boat and their father and followed him. He went around all of Galilee, teaching in their synagogues, proclaiming the gospel of the kingdom, and curing every disease and illness among the people.

Brief Silence

For Reflection

Jesus called the disciples near the beginning of his ministry. And he called them two by two, the brothers Simon and Andrew, and James and John. These were fishermen, in some ways the ancient equivalent of today's highly skilled blue-collar workers. They worked with their hands, as even the "mending their nets" indicates. At the invitation of Jesus, they all leave behind their way of life to follow him.

Modern calls to discipleship are scarcely so dramatic. But the imagery presented in Matthew speaks to us when we imagine putting away prior commitments that tend to disintegrate in the face of an invitation from Jesus. We may hear the same call to put aside the tedious, monotonous, quotidian activities that mark our lives and enter into a new relationship with him. This relationship will ultimately lead to a putting away of our entire selves, a dying to ourselves, so that we might rise with him. And that is the paschal mystery. At this, the beginning of Jesus' ministry, we hear the call to follow him to the point of forsaking our very selves. In so doing, we will be raised to new life with him.

✦ Jesus begins his preaching with the words, "Repent, for the kingdom of heaven is at hand." Where do you find the kingdom of heaven in the here and now?

Brief Silence

Prayer

Spirit of God, who calls us into relationship with Christ, give us the joy that accompanies discipleship. May we be animated by knowing the Son of God; and with such knowledge we will live our call to discipleship in good and challenging times. We ask this in the name of the triune God, who lives and reigns forever and ever. **Amen.**

On this feast of the Presentation of the Lord, we greet Christ as Anna and Simeon greeted the infant Jesus in the temple, by claiming him as our savior, our consolation, our joy. Together with them, let us draw close to Jesus and humbly ask for his healing and mercy . . .

Prayer

Our eyes have seen your salvation, Lord,
in the promise of a child given to us: Jesus, the King of glory.
Help us to recognize him in our midst.
Send us in peace, O God,
to announce what we have seen. **Amen.**

Gospel   Luke 2:22-32 (or Luke 2:22-40)

When the days were completed for their purification according to the law of Moses, / Mary and Joseph took Jesus up to Jerusalem to present him to the Lord, / just as it is written in the law of the Lord, *Every male that opens the womb shall be consecrated to the Lord,* and to offer the sacrifice of *a pair of turtledoves or two young pigeons,* in accordance with the dictate in the law of the Lord.

Now there was a man in Jerusalem whose name was Simeon. This man was righteous and devout, awaiting the consolation of Israel, and the Holy Spirit was upon him. It had been revealed to him by the Holy Spirit that he should not see death before he had seen the Christ of the Lord. He came in the Spirit into the temple; and when the parents brought in the child Jesus to perform the custom of the law in regard to him, he took him into his arms and blessed God, saying: / "Now, Master, you may let your servant go / in peace, according to your word, / for my eyes have seen your salvation, / which you prepared in sight of all the peoples, / a light for revelation to the Gentiles, / and glory for your people Israel."

Brief Silence

For Reflection

The gospel story for the presentation of the Lord is rich with theological significance and meaning. Luke gives us not only the perfunctory fulfillment of Mosaic Law, but also those actions accompanied by a prophet and by a prophetess. It should go without saying that women figure prominently in some of the most remembered stories about Jesus, including his birth, death, and resurrection. And here today we have Simeon and Anna. Many other stories about Jesus feature men so prominently that it seems only right to read today's gospel in its entirety. In so doing, we are reminded of something we know well: women speak the powerful words of God just as men do. In the Old Testament and in the New, women were prophets (prophetesses). When given the opportunity, let us showcase this too often neglected aspect of our rich faith. And in our own world, in our own day and age, let's listen attentively to the prophetesses in our own midst. Luke gives equal voice to the women. We would do well to follow his example.

✦ In Simeon and Anna we find models of faith, patience, and prophecy. How are you being called in this moment in your life to exercise the spiritual gifts of Simeon and Anna?

Brief Silence

Prayer

God of the prophets, you called those who were your own in antiquity and even up to today. Give us the grace to recognize those who speak on your behalf, so that we might have eyes to see and ears to hear. We humbly implore you. **Amen.**

In today's gospel Jesus tells us we are to be the light of the world and the salt of the earth. For the times we have failed to live up to this call, let us ask for mercy and healing . . .

Prayer

Jesus is the light of the world.
In him let our light shine before others
that all may glorify you, heavenly Father.
The light of Christ shines through the darkness;
a light for all to see. **Amen.**

Gospel   **Matt 5:13-16**

Jesus said to his disciples: "You are the salt of the earth. But if salt loses its taste, with what can it be seasoned? It is no longer good for anything but to be thrown out and trampled underfoot. You are the light of the world. A city set on a mountain cannot be hidden. Nor do they light a lamp and then put it under a bushel basket; it is set on a lampstand, where it gives light to all in the house. Just so, your light must shine before others, that they may see your good deeds and glorify your heavenly Father."

Brief Silence

For Reflection

The gospel opens with the words, "Jesus said to his disciples" thus giving us not only an account of something two thousand years ago, but something that is addressed to us today. There are two, "you are," statements that cannot be missed. The metaphors are simple but sublime: "salt" and "light." Jesus is telling his disciples as he tells us that we are the salt for the earth and the light of the world. What an impressive moniker! Are we up to it? Whether or not we deem the terms appropriate appellations, we are given those names nonetheless.

Jesus' disciples are the light of the world in that their good deeds (clothing the naked, feeding the hungry, and giving drink to the thirsty) should be seen by others. We disciples are not to do these good deeds for the sole purpose of being seen, but the deeds are to be done before others. An exemplar of this gospel passage was St. Mother Teresa whose good deeds were seen by others who in turn gave glory to God. Mother Teresa was not doing this for her own benefit. She was motivated by love; she was a "light of the world." It is our call too.

✦ When have you personally experienced works of mercy bringing "light" to your life or the lives of others?

Brief Silence

Prayer

Jesus Christ, great teacher, you call us to be salt for the earth and light for the world. Give us the dedication to live out this call daily, and when we fall short, lift us up so we can continue the journey, confident of your presence in our lives. We ask this in your holy name. **Amen.**

Today's gospel continues the Sermon on the Mount. Jesus counsels us to do more than follow the letter of the law by embodying its spirit of loving God and loving neighbor. Let us ask for God's mercy and forgiveness as we seek to keep this commandment in our own lives . . .

Prayer

Blessed are you, Father,
for you have revealed to little ones the mysteries of heaven.
Make our words true and our lives blameless in your sight.
Open our eyes that we may know
the wonders of your law, O God. **Amen.**

Gospel   Matt 5:20-22a, 27-28, 33-34a, 37 (or Matt 5:17-37)

Jesus said to his disciples: "I tell you, unless your righteousness surpasses that of the scribes and Pharisees, you will not enter the kingdom of heaven.

"You have heard that it was said to your ancestors, *You shall not kill; and whoever kills will be liable to judgment.* But I say to you, whoever is angry with his brother will be liable to judgment.

"You have heard that it was said, *You shall not commit adultery.* But I say to you, everyone who looks at a woman with lust has already committed adultery with her in his heart.

"Again you have heard that it was said to your ancestors, *Do not take a false oath, but make good to the Lord all that you vow.* But I say to you, do not swear at all. Let your 'Yes' mean 'Yes,' and your 'No' mean 'No.' Anything more is from the evil one."

Brief Silence

For Reflection

To those who want to be right with God but wonder what is the minimum required to achieve that relationship, Jesus has an answer. Jesus takes key aspects of the Law of Moses and expands them. Rather than a command not to kill, Jesus says, do not grow angry. Rather than a command not to commit adultery, Jesus says not to look at another with lust. In other words, the Mosaic Law is not simply the bare minimum we need to do to be right with God. Instead, we need to go above and beyond the letter of the Law if we are to be followers of Christ.

When Jesus responds in this way we may want a new minimum! How can I keep myself from growing angry, which is a natural human response to perceived injustice? The standard Jesus sets may seem impossible to realize. The standard established by Jesus fulfills the law rather than abolishing it. Jesus' teaching goes to the heart of the matter.

✦ These words of Jesus are straightforward and challenging, calling each of us to an examination of our own lives. Where have we let anger, lust, or dishonesty creep in? How can we instead live in a right relationship with God?

Brief Silence

Prayer

Lord Jesus, wisdom of God and teacher of the nations, you inspire us as disciples with your call to follow you. Grant us the courage to live this call even in difficult times. May we be animated by the spirit of joyful Christian discipleship in exceeding the bare minimum of your desires for us. **Amen.**

In today's readings we are called to be holy and perfect with the very holiness and perfection of God. Acknowledging our sinfulness, let us pause to ask for God's compassion and mercy . . .

Prayer

Love of neighbor is not enough, O God,
for those who live by your merciful law.
In Christ, help us to love even those we cannot.
Bless the Lord, O my soul;
with all my being, bless God's holy name. **Amen.**

Gospel   Matt 5:38-48

Jesus said to his disciples: "You have heard that it was said, *An eye for an eye and a tooth for a tooth.* But I say to you, offer no resistance to one who is evil. When someone strikes you on your right cheek, turn the other one as well. If anyone wants to go to law with you over your tunic, hand over your cloak as well. Should anyone press you into service for one mile, go for two miles. Give to the one who asks of you, and do not turn your back on one who wants to borrow.

"You have heard that it was said, *You shall love your neighbor and hate your enemy.* But I say to you, love your enemies and pray for those who persecute you, that you may be children of your heavenly Father, for he makes his sun rise on the bad and the good, and causes rain to fall on the just and the unjust. For if you love those who love you, what recompense will you have? Do not the tax collectors do the same? And if you greet your brothers only, what is unusual about that? Do not the pagans do the same? So be perfect, just as your heavenly Father is perfect."

Brief Silence

For Reflection

Admiring Jesus is easy to do. He was a gifted teacher, who lived an ethical life. His sayings inspire us, to say nothing of his death and resurrection. Yet, merely admiring Jesus is not what we are called to do. As disciples we are to follow him. The Sermon on the Mount, from which we read today, is addressed to Jesus' disciples. That is, the Sermon on the Mount is addressed to us. His words should certainly challenge us and our basic attitudes toward life. It's much easier to be evangelized by the modern culture with values of the world. And many of these values are not bad, such as treating with kindness those who treat us with kindness. But Jesus has another way. We are to pray for our persecutors. We are to turn the other cheek. In the face of such injunctions, we may choose to admire Jesus for his simple advice, while quietly concluding that is not the way the world works. Jesus would agree. He calls his disciples to be salt for the earth, leaven for the world. The conclusion of this journey is not "to get ahead" but to die on a cross. But then comes the promised resurrection.

✦ Have you had an experience in your life where you practiced Jesus' commandment, "love your enemies"? What was the outcome?

Brief Silence

Prayer

Son of God, light of the world and the way of life, you faced enemies in your time as we do in ours. Grant us patience in times of persecution and challenge, knowing that our call is to pray for those who would do us harm. May we look to you as an example of how to face adversity in our day, for you reign in heaven above. **Amen.**

On this Ash Wednesday we receive a sign of repentance. May this outward sign we bear today reflect our inner desire to return to God with our whole hearts. Acknowledging the times we have missed that mark, we pray . . .

Prayer

In this acceptable time, on this day of salvation,
create in us new hearts, O God, that we may hear your Son's voice
and turn our lives to follow your Gospel.
Blow the trumpet, and proclaim a fast,
for God is here with grace for his people. **Amen.**

Gospel   Matt 6:1-6, 16-18

Jesus said to his disciples: "Take care not to perform righteous deeds in order that people may see them; otherwise, you will have no recompense from your heavenly Father. When you give alms, do not blow a trumpet before you, as the hypocrites do in the synagogues and in the streets to win the praise of others. Amen, I say to you, they have received their reward. But when you give alms, do not let your left hand know what your right is doing, so that your almsgiving may be secret. And your Father who sees in secret will repay you.

"When you pray, do not be like the hypocrites, who love to stand and pray in the synagogues and on street corners so that others may see them. Amen, I say to you, they have received their reward. But when you pray, go to your inner room, close the door, and pray to your Father in secret. And your Father who sees in secret will repay you.

"When you fast, do not look gloomy like the hypocrites. They neglect their appearance, so that they may appear to others to be fasting. Amen, I say to you, they have received their reward. But when you fast, anoint your head and wash your face, so that you may not appear to be fasting, except to your Father who is hidden. And your Father who sees what is hidden will repay you."

Brief Silence

For Reflection

Jesus' own teaching in the Sermon on the Mount is on par with and fulfills the Mosaic Law. His lessons apply equally to the audience of his day as they do to us today. The three marks of our Lenten season—almsgiving, prayer, and fasting—are the objects of Jesus' teaching.

There can be a temptation for any religious person to be seen as religious, pleasing to God, and therefore pleasing to others. These sorts of people were prevalent in Jesus' day, as they are in our own. Such actors are "hypocrites" in the eyes of Jesus or, more literally translated, "stage actors." The disciples of Jesus are told that the true audience of their almsgiving, prayer, and fasting is God, not fellow human beings. The disciples are certainly to give alms, fast, and pray, but not to make a show of it.

Disciples are to give alms "in secret." Some in Jesus' day would toss coins in the street for the poor, making a show of their own generosity. Such "generous" figures already received their reward by being the object of praise by others. Far better to give secretly; the audience (God in heaven) knows what we do.

✦ How are you being called to live the Lenten disciplines of almsgiving, prayer, and fasting?

Brief Silence

Prayer

Lord God, giver of life who calls us to be with you eternally, make us mindful of our ultimate destiny, so that our choices in life may be made with this in mind. When a desire to accumulate earthly treasures grows in us, inspire us instead to store up riches in heaven, where we will be with you and all those we love for eternity. In your name we pray. **Amen.**

In today's first reading we hear of how God formed Adam from the clay of the ground and then "blew into his nostrils the breath of life." For the times that our lives have not reflected the life of God, let us ask for pardon and mercy . . .

Prayer

Free us, O God, from the temptation
of not believing in our hearts what we sing with our mouths,
for the Word you speak is living bread for the hungry.
O Lord, open my lips,
and my mouth shall proclaim your praise. **Amen.**

Gospel   Matt 4:1-11

At that time Jesus was led by the Spirit into the desert to be tempted by the devil. He fasted for forty days and forty nights, and afterwards he was hungry. The tempter approached and said to him, "If you are the Son of God, command that these stones become loaves of bread." He said in reply, "It is written: / *One does not live on bread alone, / but on every word that comes forth / from the mouth of God.*"

Then the devil took him to the holy city, and made him stand on the parapet of the temple, and said to him, "If you are the Son of God, throw yourself down. For it is written: / *He will command his angels concerning you / and with their hands they will support you, / lest you dash your foot against a stone.*" / Jesus answered him, "Again it is written, *You shall not put the Lord, your God, to the test.*" Then the devil took him up to a very high mountain, and showed him all the kingdoms of the world in their magnificence, and he said to him, "All these I shall give to you, if you will prostrate yourself and worship me." At this, Jesus said to him, "Get away, Satan! It is written: / *The Lord, your God, shall you worship / and him alone shall you serve."*

Then the devil left him and, behold, angels came and ministered to him.

Brief Silence

For Reflection

In today's gospel we learn that Jesus himself faced temptation, and not only one but three. The early church fathers recognized that these temptations were metaphorical for (1) the needs of the body, (2) one's relationship with the divine, and (3) one's own desire for power and glory. In each instance, of course, Jesus overcomes the temptation. He recognizes that one does not live on bread alone, that one does not put the Lord to the test, and that power and glory are not to be had by worshiping anything other than God.

If these temptations seem beyond us, we need only look more carefully at our own lives. Temptation does not approach us as the devil incarnate. Christians have known this for centuries. The story in Matthew's gospel was meant to be understood broadly, addressing fundamental temptations of humankind for the self. In those circumstances, we rest in our baptism, knowing that our relationship with God is secure. As disciples of Christ, we are confident sons and daughters of God.

✦ In the desert Jesus is tempted to sate his hunger, test God's love for him, and rule the kingdoms of the world by worshiping the devil. Which of these temptations (material goods, testing God, power and glory) is the one you struggle with the most?

Brief Silence

Prayer

Our Father in heaven, your son Jesus taught us to pray that we may not be led into temptation. Keep our minds and hearts focused solely on you, and when we do face opportunities to choose another path, give us the grace to choose you. We ask this as disciples of your son, who taught us about you. **Amen.**

In today's gospel Peter, James, and John hear a voice from a cloud tell them, "This is my beloved Son, with whom I am well pleased; / listen to him." Let us pause to ask for God's mercy for the times we have not been attentive to his voice . . .

Prayer

Lord, it is good that we are here to sing your praise.
But teach us to follow you even to the cross
that not by works but by your grace we may be saved.
Let your mercy be on us, O God,
as we place our trust in you. **Amen.**

Gospel   **Matt 17:1-9**

Jesus took Peter, James, and John his brother, and led them up a high mountain by themselves. And he was transfigured before them; his face shone like the sun and his clothes became white as light. And behold, Moses and Elijah appeared to them, conversing with him. Then Peter said to Jesus in reply, "Lord, it is good that we are here. If you wish, I will make three tents here, one for you, one for Moses, and one for Elijah." While he was still speaking, behold, a bright cloud cast a shadow over them, then from the cloud came a voice that said, "This is my beloved Son, with whom I am well pleased; listen to him." When the disciples heard this, they fell prostrate and were very much afraid. But Jesus came and touched them, saying, "Rise, and do not be afraid." And when the disciples raised their eyes, they saw no one else but Jesus alone.

As they were coming down from the mountain, Jesus charged them, "Do not tell the vision to anyone until the Son of Man has been raised from the dead."

Brief Silence

For Reflection

The church gives us Matthew's story of the transfiguration, which foretells the resurrection, on this Second Sunday of Lent. The Lenten season will culminate with Triduum and then Easter Sunday. The transfiguration gives the disciples and us a foretaste of the kingdom, and a reminder of Jesus' divine glory.

Moses and Elijah represent the Law and the Prophets. These two majestic figures in Israelite history each received a revelation from God on Mount Horeb (Sinai). Together they stand as pillars of Judaism, which Jesus himself fulfills.

This remarkable event surely emboldened the disciples in their faith, while it also seized them with fear. This mountaintop experience meant even more after the resurrection when the words of Jesus became clear.

The gospel today reminds us of our ultimate end, which is to be with Jesus in the heavenly realm. With such knowledge, cares of the world may wash away. Even a desire to commemorate such an event, as Peter desired to build three tents, is as nothing when compared to the experience itself. We have a foreshadowing of eternal glory. Let us continue to follow Jesus down the mountain, learning from him the entire way, knowing that the ultimate resurrection requires undergoing death itself.

✦ On the mountaintop the disciples hear a voice from the cloud proclaiming, "This is my beloved Son, with whom I am well pleased; / listen to him." In prayer, how do you spend time listening to God?

Brief Silence

Prayer

Lord Jesus, you fulfilled the Law and the Prophets. You were transfigured from death into new life and now you live and reign in heaven above. We believe you are God's beloved son and we strive to listen to you. Grant us ears to hear your voice in the midst of our world. In your name we pray. **Amen.**

In today's gospel the Samaritan woman tells her townspeople that Jesus "told me everything I have done." Let us turn to the one who knows all of our thoughts and deeds, both those that are charitable and righteous and those that are not, and ask for pardon and mercy . . .

Prayer

Lord Jesus, you are truly the Savior of the world.
Soften our hardened hearts in the springs of eternal life
that we may hear your word and announce your salvation.
Come, let us sing joyfully to the Lord;
let us acclaim the Rock of our salvation. **Amen.**

Gospel **John 4:5-15, 19b-26, 39a, 40-42 (or John 4:5-42)**

Jesus came to a town of Samaria called Sychar, near the plot of land that Jacob had given to his son Joseph. Jacob's well was there. Jesus, tired from his journey, sat down there at the well. It was about noon.

A woman of Samaria came to draw water. Jesus said to her, "Give me a drink." His disciples had gone into the town to buy food. The Samaritan woman said to him, "How can you, a Jew, ask me, a Samaritan woman, for a drink?"—For Jews use nothing in common with Samaritans.—Jesus answered and said to her, "If you knew the gift of God and who is saying to you, 'Give me a drink,' you would have asked him and he would have given you living water." The woman said to him, "Sir, you do not even have a bucket and the cistern is deep; where then can you get this living water? Are you greater than our father Jacob, who gave us this cistern and drank from it himself with his children and his flocks?" Jesus answered and said to her, "Everyone who drinks this water will be thirsty again; but whoever drinks the water I shall give will never thirst; the water I shall give will become in him a spring of water welling up to eternal life." The woman said to him, "Sir, give me this water, so that I may not be thirsty or have to keep coming here to draw water.

"I can see that you are a prophet. Our ancestors worshiped on this mountain; but you people say that the place to worship is in Jerusalem." Jesus said to her, "Believe me, woman, the hour is coming when you will worship the Father neither on this mountain nor in Jerusalem. You people worship what you do not understand; we worship what we understand, because salvation is from the Jews. But the hour is coming, and is now here, when true worshipers will worship the Father in Spirit and truth; and indeed the Father seeks such people to worship him. God is Spirit, and those who worship him must worship in Spirit and truth." The woman said to him, "I know that the Messiah is coming, the one called the Christ; when he comes, he will tell us everything." Jesus said to her, "I am he, the one who is speaking with you."

Many of the Samaritans of that town began to believe in him. When the Samaritans came to him, they invited him to stay with them; and he stayed there two days. Many more began to believe in him because of his word, and they said to the woman, "We no longer believe because of your word; for we have heard for ourselves, and we know that this is truly the savior of the world."

Brief Silence

For Reflection

Today we accompany Jesus as he meets the woman at the well. Samaritans were not considered by Judeans to be truly Jewish, as they worshipped not at the temple (which was in Judea) but at Shechem ("on this mountain"). Jesus tells the woman that there will come a time (considered fulfilled at the time of the writing of the Gospel of John) "when true worshipers will worship the Father in Spirit and truth." No longer will it matter whether one is at a particular place for worship.

The woman recognizes that Jesus is a prophet, and Jesus himself eventually reveals to her that he is the Messiah, the Christ. Even so, she does not initially refer to him with that title herself. Instead, she goes back to her townspeople claiming that she met someone who could be the Christ. Because of her word, many of the townspeople believed in him. After Jesus stayed with them for some time, many more came to believe in him, hearing him for themselves. They then claim to know that "he is the savior of the world."

Thus we have a gradual coming to faith in the encounter at the well, a model for countless generations of disciples ever since.

✦ Through the Samaritan woman's witness, her townspeople welcome Jesus into their village and eventually come to believe he is the savior of the world. In your life of faith, who have been the witnesses who have led you to relationship with Christ?

Brief Silence

Prayer

Lord Jesus, you were recognized as prophet and Messiah by the woman at the well. Her testimony led many others to faith. May we have the spirit of evangelization, sharing our experience of you with others, so that this may lead others to faith. We have come to believe you are the savior of the world. Through this belief we have life in your name. **Amen.**

In today's second reading, St. Paul urges the Ephesians to "[l]ive as children of light." As we begin this celebration let us bring our sins and failings before the Lord, trusting in his mercy, love, and healing light . . .

Prayer

Lord Jesus, you are the Light of the world.
Anoint our eyes with your merciful gaze
that we may be healed of our blindness and see one another with
　　　your love.
The Lord is my shepherd;
there is nothing I shall want. **Amen.**

Gospel   John 9:1, 6-9, 13-17, 34-38 (or John 9:1-41)

As Jesus passed by he saw a man blind from birth. He spat on the ground and made clay with the saliva, and smeared the clay on his eyes, and said to him, "Go wash in the Pool of Siloam"—which means Sent—. So he went and washed, and came back able to see.

His neighbors and those who had seen him earlier as a beggar said, "Isn't this the one who used to sit and beg?" Some said, "It is," but others said, "No, he just looks like him." He said, "I am."

They brought the one who was once blind to the Pharisees. Now Jesus had made clay and opened his eyes on a sabbath. So then the Pharisees also asked him how he was able to see. He said to them, "He put clay on my eyes, and I washed, and now I can see." So some of the Pharisees said, "This man is not from God, because he does not keep the sabbath." But others said, "How can a sinful man do such signs?" And there was a division among them. So they said to the blind man again, "What do you have to say about him, since he opened your eyes?" He said, "He is a prophet."

They answered and said to him, "You were born totally in sin, and are you trying to teach us?" Then they threw him out.

When Jesus heard that they had thrown him out, he found him and said, "Do you believe in the Son of Man?" He answered and said, "Who is he, sir, that I may believe in him?" Jesus said to him, "You have seen him, and the one speaking with you is he." He said, "I do believe, Lord," and he worshiped him.

Brief Silence

For Reflection

This week, Jesus heals the man born blind. The story is masterfully and artfully complex yet succinct. Drama abounds and intrigue develops with each verse.

The story opens with popular wisdom of the day expressed by the disciples. "Whose fault is it?" that the man is blind. Jesus rejects such attribution. It is not that bad things happen to bad people. Such thinking, which infects many religious and non-religious people, is not new in our own day. Jesus is far removed from any "prosperity gospel" (good things happen to those who are good), as it might be understood today.

In today's story, Jesus takes the initiative. He creates cognitive dissonance in the minds and hearts of many, demanding that they make a decision for or against him. When do we face such encounters with Christ? What is our response? Do we deny what everyone can plainly see? Or do we undergo a change and enter into a new life with Christ?

✦ In your life of faith, when have you had an experience of conversion or suddenly being able to "see" where before you had a spiritual "blind spot"?

Brief Silence

Prayer

Jesus Christ, light of the world, you made the blind man see. Give us vision to see the world as you do, to recognize injustice and subsequently work to overcome it. May your light shine in our world, and may we too reflect this same light in our lives. In your name we pray. **Amen.**

On this Fifth Sunday of Lent, we journey with Jesus to Bethany where he will raise his friend Lazarus from the dead. Let us bring before the Lord all the places in our own lives that are in need of his life-giving touch . . .

Prayer

Lord Jesus, you are the resurrection and the life.
Still you weep with us when we weep at death's door.
Strengthen our faith to believe in you always.
I trust in the Lord;
my soul trusts in God's word. **Amen.**

Gospel   **John 11:3-7, 17, 20-27, 33b-45 (or John 11:1-45)**

The sisters of Lazarus sent word to Jesus, saying, "Master, the one you love is ill." When Jesus heard this he said, "This illness is not to end in death, but is for the glory of God, that the Son of God may be glorified through it." Now Jesus loved Martha and her sister and Lazarus. So when he heard that he was ill, he remained for two days in the place where he was. Then after this he said to his disciples, "Let us go back to Judea."

When Jesus arrived, he found that Lazarus had already been in the tomb for four days. When Martha heard that Jesus was coming, she went to meet him; but Mary sat at home. Martha said to Jesus, "Lord, if you had been here, my brother would not have died. But even now I know that whatever you ask of God, God will give you." Jesus said to her, "Your brother will rise." Martha said, "I know he will rise, in the resurrection on the last day." Jesus told her, "I am the resurrection and the life; whoever believes in me, even if he dies, will live, and everyone who lives and believes in me will never die. Do you believe this?" She said to him, "Yes, Lord. I have come to believe that you are the Christ, the Son of God, the one who is coming into the world."

He became perturbed and deeply troubled, and said, "Where have you laid him?" They said to him, "Sir, come and see." And Jesus wept. So the Jews said, "See how he loved him." But some of them said, "Could not the one who opened the eyes of the blind man have done something so that this man would not have died?"

So Jesus, perturbed again, came to the tomb. It was a cave, and a stone lay across it. Jesus said, "Take away the stone." Martha, the dead man's sister, said to him, "Lord, by now there will be a stench; he has been dead for four days." Jesus said to her, "Did I not tell you that if you believe you will see the glory of God?" So they took away the stone. And Jesus raised his eyes and said, "Father, I thank you for hearing me. I know that you always hear me; but because of the crowd here I have said this, that they may believe that you sent me." And when he had said this, he cried out in a loud voice, "Lazarus, come out!" The dead man came out, tied hand and foot with burial bands, and his face was wrapped in a cloth. So Jesus said to them, "Untie him and let him go."

Now many of the Jews who had come to Mary and seen what he had done began to believe in him.

Brief Silence

For Reflection

Today's gospel story is filled with misunderstanding, which itself functions as a narrative device that the evangelist uses to illustrate how Jesus' thoughts and ways of knowing are so beyond that of the disciples'. For example, the disciples understood Jesus literally in thinking that Lazarus was only asleep. Jesus then tells them plainly that "Lazarus has died." He expresses gratitude that he was not there so that the disciples can believe (when he raises Lazarus from the dead). But even this is misunderstood by Thomas, who believes they are going to die with Jesus.

The misunderstanding continues with Martha's gentle scolding of Jesus when she claims that had Jesus been present, Lazarus would not have died. We recall that Jesus waited for two days after hearing the news of Lazarus being sick before he even went to see him! Jesus instead proclaims himself the resurrection and life. Martha, in another case of misunderstanding, says she knows that Lazarus will rise on the last day. (She does not understand that Jesus will raise him shortly.)

Jesus' prayer to the Father is fundamentally one of thanksgiving and gratitude for the opportunity for those gathered to believe that Jesus is sent by God the Father. His ways are far above those of ours.

✦ Jesus reveals to Martha, "I am the resurrection and the life." How do you interpret these words?

Brief Silence

Prayer

Lord Jesus, you are the resurrection and the life. You give meaning to our existence and you give hope to an eternal future. Your ways are far above our own, so we ask for the grace to live as your disciples in the midst of the world, confident of our destiny to be with you and those we love for all eternity. **Amen.**

Today we gather to enter into the passion of the Lord and to bear witness to the moment of his death on a cross. Let us pause to seek God's mercy and healing that through this remembrance of the Lord's passion and death, we might be brought to the fullness of life . . .

Prayer

As we enter the Mystery of this sacred time,
grant us, Lord, a well-trained tongue,
that we might speak and sing a word to rouse the weary heart.
I will proclaim your name to my people;
in the midst of the assembly I will praise you. **Amen.**

Gospel   Matt 27:11-54

Jesus stood before the governor, Pontius Pilate, who questioned him, "Are you the king of the Jews?" Jesus said, "You say so." And when he was accused by the chief priests and elders, he made no answer. Then Pilate said to him, "Do you not hear how many things they are testifying against you?" But he did not answer him one word, so that the governor was greatly amazed.

Now on the occasion of the feast the governor was accustomed to release to the crowd one prisoner whom they wished. And at that time they had a notorious prisoner called Barabbas. So when they had assembled, Pilate said to them, "Which one do you want me to release to you, Barabbas, or Jesus called Christ?" For he knew that it was out of envy that they had handed him over. While he was still seated on the bench, his wife sent him a message, "Have nothing to do with that righteous man. I suffered much in a dream today because of him." The chief priests and the elders persuaded the crowds to ask for Barabbas but to destroy Jesus. The governor said to them in reply, "Which of the two do you want me to release to you?" They answered, "Barabbas!" Pilate said to them, "Then what shall I do with Jesus called Christ?" They all said, "Let him be crucified!" But he said, "Why? What evil has he done?" They only shouted the louder, "Let him be crucified!" When Pilate saw that he was not succeeding at all, but that a riot was breaking out instead, he took water and washed his hands in the sight of the crowd, saying, "I am innocent of this man's blood. Look to it yourselves." And the whole people said in reply, "His blood be upon us and upon our children." Then he released Barabbas to them, but after he had Jesus scourged, he handed him over to be crucified.

Then the soldiers of the governor took Jesus inside the praetorium and gathered the whole cohort around him. They stripped off his clothes and threw a scarlet military cloak about him. Weaving a crown out of thorns, they placed it on his head, and a reed in his right hand. And kneeling before him, they mocked him, saying, "Hail, King of the Jews!" They spat upon him and took the reed and kept striking him on the head. And when they had mocked him, they stripped him of the cloak, dressed him in his own clothes, and led him off to crucify him.

As they were going out, they met a Cyrenian named Simon; this man they pressed into service to carry his cross.

And when they came to a place called Golgotha—which means Place of the Skull—, they gave Jesus wine to drink mixed with gall. But when he had tasted it, he refused to drink. After they had crucified him, they divided his garments by casting lots; then they sat down and kept watch over him there. And they placed over his head the written charge against him: This is Jesus, the King of the Jews. Two revolutionaries were crucified with him, one on his right and the other on his left. Those passing by reviled him, shaking their heads and saying, "You who would destroy the temple and rebuild it in three days, save yourself, if you are the Son of

God, and come down from the cross!" Likewise the chief priests with the scribes and elders mocked him and said, "He saved others; he cannot save himself. So he is the king of Israel! Let him come down from the cross now, and we will believe in him. He trusted in God; let him deliver him now if he wants him. For he said, 'I am the Son of God.'" The revolutionaries who were crucified with him also kept abusing him in the same way.

From noon onward, darkness came over the whole land until three in the afternoon. And about three o'clock Jesus cried out in a loud voice, *"Eli, Eli, lema sabachthani?"* which means, "My God, my God, why have you forsaken me?" Some of the bystanders who heard it said, "This one is calling for Elijah." Immediately one of them ran to get a sponge; he soaked it in wine, and putting it on a reed, gave it to him to drink. But the rest said, "Wait, let us see if Elijah comes to save him." But Jesus cried out again in a loud voice, and gave up his spirit.

Here all kneel and pause for a short time.

And behold, the veil of the sanctuary was torn in two from top to bottom. The earth quaked, rocks were split, tombs were opened, and the bodies of many saints who had fallen asleep were raised. And coming forth from their tombs after his resurrection, they entered the holy city and appeared to many. The centurion and the men with him who were keeping watch over Jesus feared greatly when they saw the earthquake and all that was happening, and they said, "Truly, this was the Son of God!"

Brief Silence

For Reflection

Palm Sunday is a commemoration of highs and lows, exaltation and tragedy. We enter the church bearing palms singing Hosanna, and only minutes later we cry in unison, "Let him be crucified." The liturgical juxtaposition is certainly intended and representative of fickle humanity. Profound themes of betrayal, trust, friendship, power, and humility are present in the gospel reading from Matthew.

Who doesn't know what it's like to experience betrayal at the hand of a friend, for that is the very term Jesus uses of Judas Iscariot? Judas himself leads the authorities to Jesus for the price of thirty pieces of silver, only to commit suicide hours later. He was dead before Jesus was. Peter, too, betrayed Jesus. The disciples who professed such devotion to Jesus only hours earlier folded quickly in the face of temptation. Jesus died alone, reviled even by those who were being crucified alongside him.

Of course, to be God's son means that Jesus trusts the Father to the point of enduring all things up to and including death. God's vindication will come not in bringing Jesus down from the cross, but in raising Jesus from the dead. God's ways are not human ways.

✦ Throughout the Lenten season we have prepared to enter into Holy Week by our practices of prayer, fasting, and almsgiving. How have your Lenten practices strengthened and nourished you this Lent?

Brief Silence

Prayer

Lord Jesus, you were unjustly condemned and put to death by the power of the state. May we place our hope not in human rulers but in you alone. May we be prepared to speak on behalf of those who face injustice. Give us the grace to see your face in those who suffer today. In your name we pray. **Amen.**

With this celebration we enter into the holiest days of our Christian year. Let us pause to ask for God's mercy and healing as we seek to keep the Sacred Paschal Triduum with devotion and grace . . .

Prayer

You give us a new commandment, Lord,
to love one another as you loved us.
May your paschal mystery shape us ever more into your likeness.
Let us offer our sacrifice of praise
for all the good God has done for us. **Amen.**

Gospel   **John 13:1-15**

Before the feast of Passover, Jesus knew that his hour had come to pass from this world to the Father. He loved his own in the world and he loved them to the end. The devil had already induced Judas, son of Simon the Iscariot, to hand him over. So, during supper, fully aware that the Father had put everything into his power and that he had come from God and was returning to God, he rose from supper and took off his outer garments. He took a towel and tied it around his waist. Then he poured water into a basin and began to wash the disciples' feet and dry them with the towel around his waist. He came to Simon Peter, who said to him, "Master, are you going to wash my feet?" Jesus answered and said to him, "What I am doing, you do not understand now, but you will understand later." Peter said to him, "You will never wash my feet." Jesus answered him, "Unless I wash you, you will have no inheritance with me." Simon Peter said to him, "Master, then not only my feet, but my hands and head as well." Jesus said to him, "Whoever has bathed has no need except to have his feet washed, for he is clean all over; so you are clean, but not all." For he knew who would betray him; for this reason, he said, "Not all of you are clean."

So when he had washed their feet and put his garments back on and reclined at table again, he said to them, "Do you realize what I have done for you? You call me 'teacher' and 'master,' and rightly so, for indeed I am. If I, therefore, the master and teacher, have washed your feet, you ought to wash one another's feet. I have given you a model to follow, so that as I have done for you, you should also do."

Brief Silence

For Reflection

To celebrate this Mass of the Lord's Supper, which commemorates the last meal Jesus had with his disciples, we read from the Gospel of John, which has a unique timeline for the event. The opening words of this gospel are often overlooked, but they indicate something critical. "Before the feast of Passover" tells the reader that this is not a Passover meal. The Synoptic Gospels, on the other hand, tell us that the Last Supper was a Passover meal. But in the Gospel of John, Jesus is dead by Passover. These two chronologies cannot be reconciled; ultimately the gospels convey theology rather than history. In fact, according to John's chronology, Jesus (the Lamb of God) is crucified at about the time the lambs are being slaughtered in preparation for the Passover meal later that evening. John is the only evangelist to use the title "Lamb of God" for Jesus, and it illustrates his unique theological perspective. Therefore, perhaps counterintuitively, there is no "institution of the Eucharist" during the Last Supper in this gospel. Instead, Jesus gives his disciples an outward sign of service, which they are to do also: wash one another's feet. Christian identity is marked by service. As Jesus the master has done, so should we also do.

✦ In tonight's gospel Jesus gives us a model of service. When in the past year have you been served by others? When have you been the servant?

Brief Silence

HOLY THURSDAY EVENING MASS OF THE LORD'S SUPPER

Prayer

Jesus, you are the bread of life, food for a world that desperately needs you. In gratitude for your gift of the Eucharist, we commit ourselves to follow your example and feed the hungry, give drink to the thirsty, and clothe the naked. By these acts in imitation of you, we live our discipleship and your call to do the Father's will. **Amen.**

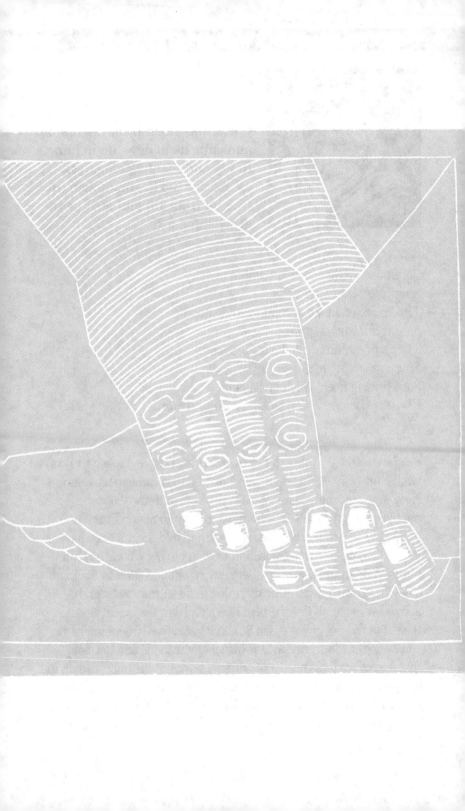

Christ has risen from the tomb and calls us to new life in him. In joy and thanksgiving, let us ask for his healing touch to free us from sin and lead us to everlasting life . . .

Prayer

Christians, to the Paschal Lamb:
Sing your thankful praises!
The Prince of Life has conquered death:
Sing your thankful praises!
The empty tomb is filled with blessing:
Sing your thankful praises!
For Christ is risen! Alleluia! Alleluia!
Christ is risen indeed! Alleluia! Alleluia! **Amen.**

Gospel   **John 20:1-9 (or Matt 28:1-10 or Luke 24:13-35)**

On the first day of the week, Mary of Magdala came to the tomb early in the morning, while it was still dark, and saw the stone removed from the tomb. So she ran and went to Simon Peter and to the other disciple whom Jesus loved, and told them, "They have taken the Lord from the tomb, and we don't know where they put him." So Peter and the other disciple went out and came to the tomb. They both ran, but the other disciple ran faster than Peter and arrived at the tomb first; he bent down and saw the burial cloths there, but did not go in. When Simon Peter arrived after him, he went into the tomb and saw the burial cloths there, and the cloth that had covered his head, not with the burial cloths but rolled up in a separate place. Then the other disciple also went in, the one who had arrived at the tomb first, and he saw and believed. For they did not yet understand the Scripture that he had to rise from the dead.

Brief Silence

For Reflection

That first Easter morning must have been a whirlwind of confusion, perplexity, and ultimately joy. According to John's gospel, Mary of Magdala was the first to find the tomb empty. Her reaction was not belief in the resurrection, but something more banal—that somebody had stolen the body. She immediately informs Peter and another disciple of her suspicion. That other disciple, thought to be the Beloved Disciple ("the disciple whom he [Jesus] loved"), is nameless throughout the Gospel of John. He is portrayed as the model of discipleship, as "he saw and believed," something not even Peter did upon witnessing the empty tomb.

Interestingly, the gospel passage ends on the note that these disciples did not yet understand the Scripture that he had to rise from the dead. After all this time with Jesus, and even finding the tomb empty, they still did not understand. Yet, the Beloved Disciple, at least, believed. Such a story gives hope to us who did not travel with Jesus or experience his historical ministry. If we have questions or experience a lack of understanding, we may be assured that the earliest disciples, the followers of Jesus himself, felt the same way even after the resurrection.

✦ In the gospel we are told that upon entering the tomb, the Beloved Disciple "saw and believed." What has been your own journey to belief in the resurrection?

Brief Silence

Prayer

Christ almighty, you rose from the dead giving hope to the living. Your life is light for the world and a promise of present and future joy. May the experience of Easter inform our understanding of the world, so that we know death leads to life, loss leads to gain, and sorrow leads to consolation. You upend the ways of the world with the ways of God. For this we praise and thank you. **Amen.**

In today's gospel the risen Christ appears to his disciples and offers them his peace. May these waters cleanse, purify, and strengthen us to bear Christ's peace to others . . .

Prayer

Give thanks to the Lord, for God is good:
God's mercy endures forever!
Let all that has breath sing praise to God:
God's mercy endures forever!
God casts all fear and doubt away:
God's mercy endures forever!
Christ is risen! Alleluia! Alleluia!
Christ is risen indeed! Alleluia! Alleluia! **Amen.**

Gospel   John 20:19-31

On the evening of that first day of the week, when the doors were locked, where the disciples were, for fear of the Jews, Jesus came and stood in their midst and said to them, "Peace be with you." When he had said this, he showed them his hands and his side. The disciples rejoiced when they saw the Lord. Jesus said to them again, "Peace be with you. As the Father has sent me, so I send you." And when he had said this, he breathed on them and said to them, "Receive the Holy Spirit. Whose sins you forgive are forgiven them, and whose sins you retain are retained."

Thomas, called Didymus, one of the Twelve, was not with them when Jesus came. So the other disciples said to him, "We have seen the Lord." But he said to them, "Unless I see the mark of the nails in his hands and put my finger into the nailmarks and put my hand into his side, I will not believe."

Now a week later his disciples were again inside and Thomas was with them. Jesus came, although the doors were locked, and stood in their midst and said, "Peace be with you." Then he said to Thomas, "Put your finger here and see my hands, and bring your hand and put it into my side, and do not be unbelieving, but believe." Thomas answered and said to him, "My Lord and my God!" Jesus said to him, "Have you come to believe because you have seen me? Blessed are those who have not seen and have believed."

Now, Jesus did many other signs in the presence of his disciples that are not written in this book. But these are written that you may come to believe that Jesus is the Christ, the Son of God, and that through this belief you may have life in his name.

Brief Silence

For Reflection

On this the Second Sunday of Easter the church gives us the only gospel reading that corresponds to the week after Easter, namely the story of "Doubting Thomas" (though he is never called that in the story). On the evening of Easter Sunday, Jesus makes his appearance to the disciples, though Thomas is absent. It is only one week later when Jesus appears again. During this intervening week, we might wonder what the other disciples said to Thomas, and we might wonder at Thomas's obstinacy in the face of their witness. Not only had Thomas experienced Jesus throughout his earthly ministry, but Thomas had the eyewitness testimony of his fellow disciples, his friends. Still, his lack of belief persisted. Only a personal experience of the risen Christ would melt away his doubt and unbelief. Such is a model of how individuals come to faith. Sometimes, like Thomas, despite all the evidence, testimony, and enthusiasm of believers, faith will never take root unless one personally encounters the risen Christ. Still, Jesus utters a beatitude that is meant for us, the reader: "Blessed are those who have not seen and have believed."

✦ Thomas believes in the resurrection only after seeing the risen Christ. Jesus tells him, "Blessed are those who have not seen and have believed." What are the events or experiences in your life that have brought you to belief?

Brief Silence

Prayer

Son of God, hope for the world, you showed yourself alive after the resurrection and yet there were still some who doubted. When we have moments of doubt ourselves may we call to mind your disciples who lived fidelity in the face of such hesitation. The totality of their lives overcame any particular shortcoming in a moment of distress. Though we want to be model disciples at all times, when we fall short, shower us with your grace and mercy ever more. For we rely on your goodness and kindness. **Amen.**

In today's gospel, two disciples recognize Jesus in the breaking of the bread. As we prepare to draw close to Jesus at the eucharistic feast, may this water remind us of the waters of baptism as they cleanse and restore us . . .

Prayer

By encountering the stranger on the way,
you heal our grief, O God.
By inviting them to stay with us,
you make the cold night warm and safe.
In the breaking of the bread,
you feed our hearts with hope.
You will show us the path to life. Alleluia!
Abounding joy in your presence. Alleluia! **Amen.**

Gospel   Luke 24:13-35

That very day, the first day of the week, two of Jesus' disciples were going to a village seven miles from Jerusalem called Emmaus, and they were conversing about all the things that had occurred. And it happened that while they were conversing and debating, Jesus himself drew near and walked with them, but their eyes were prevented from recognizing him. He asked them, "What are you discussing as you walk along?" They stopped, looking downcast. One of them, named Cleopas, said to him in reply, "Are you the only visitor to Jerusalem who does not know of the things that have taken place there in these days?" And he replied to them, "What sort of things?" They said to him, "The things that happened to Jesus the Nazarene, who was a prophet mighty in deed and word before God and all the people, how our chief priests and rulers both handed him over to a sentence of death and crucified him. But we were hoping that he would be the one to redeem Israel; and besides all this, it is now the third day since this took place. Some women from our group, however, have astounded us: they were at the tomb early in the morning and did not find his body; they came back and reported that they had indeed seen a vision of angels who announced that he was alive. Then some of those with us went to the tomb and found things just as the women had described, but him they did not see." And he said to them, "Oh, how foolish you are! How slow of heart to believe all that the prophets spoke! Was it not necessary that the Christ should suffer these things and enter into his glory?" Then beginning with Moses and all the prophets, he interpreted to them what referred to him in all the Scriptures. As they approached the village to which they were going, he gave the impression that he was going on farther. But they urged him, "Stay with us, for it is nearly evening and the day is almost over." So he went in to stay with them. And it happened that, while he was with them at table, he took bread, said the blessing, broke it, and gave it to them. With that their eyes were opened and they recognized him, but he vanished from their sight. Then they said to each other, "Were not our hearts burning within us while he spoke to us on the way and opened the Scriptures to us?" So they set out at once and returned to Jerusalem where they found gathered together the eleven and those with them who were saying, "The Lord has truly been raised and has appeared to Simon!" Then the two recounted what had taken place on the way and how he was made known to them in the breaking of the bread.

Brief Silence

For Reflection

After Easter, the disciples come to know Jesus in the breaking of the bread. With this experience, the two disciples race back to Jerusalem to report their encounter to the assembled others. The two are told that Jesus has also appeared to Simon, which according to Luke's gospel was the first appearance. The experience of coming to know him in the breaking of the bread is additional confirmation that Jesus lives eternally, building on the appearance of the risen Christ to Simon. He is present among his followers as he was prior to his death and resurrection, but now, he is present in a new way.

Of course, as Catholics, we see this clearly in the Eucharist, when we take bread, bless it, break it, and give it. The bread broken is Christ himself. He is our nourishment both spiritually and physically, metaphorically and actually. When we participate in the Eucharist, we call to mind his passion, death, and resurrection. We consume him who is the Bread of Life. When we want to know Jesus, we experience the Eucharist not merely by gazing at it, but by consuming it—for it is real food.

✦ The disciples describe their interaction with Jesus as one that caused their hearts to burn within them. What spiritual practices bring you closer to Jesus?

Brief Silence

Prayer

Jesus Christ, you have been raised into glory and we now come to know you in the breaking of the bread. May we imitate the example you set for us, and become broken in service to the least among us. In our living discipleship may we emulate the values you came to teach us. Nourished by you in the Eucharist, we become empowered to do your work on earth. In your name we pray. **Amen.**

In today's gospel reading Jesus proclaims that he is the gate of the sheepfold through which we are saved. May this water remind us of the waters of baptism and our own birth into the sheepfold of the church . . .

Prayer

When we fear we do not have enough,
Good Shepherd, guide us.
When we doubt our own worth,
Good Shepherd, encourage us.
When we believe we are alone,
Good Shepherd, call to us.
The Lord is my shepherd. Alleluia!
There is nothing I shall want. Alleluia! **Amen.**

Gospel   John 10:1-10

Jesus said: "Amen, amen, I say to you, whoever does not enter a sheepfold through the gate but climbs over elsewhere is a thief and a robber. But whoever enters through the gate is the shepherd of the sheep. The gatekeeper opens it for him, and the sheep hear his voice, as the shepherd calls his own sheep by name and leads them out. When he has driven out all his own, he walks ahead of them, and the sheep follow him, because they recognize his voice. But they will not follow a stranger; they will run away from him, because they do not recognize the voice of strangers." Although Jesus used this figure of speech, the Pharisees did not realize what he was trying to tell them.

So Jesus said again, "Amen, amen, I say to you, I am the gate for the sheep. All who came before me are thieves and robbers, but the sheep did not listen to them. I am the gate. Whoever enters through me will be saved, and will come in and go out and find pasture. A thief comes only to steal and slaughter and destroy; I came so that they might have life and have it more abundantly."

Brief Silence

For Reflection

In the "figure of speech" in today's gospel, we are sheep whereas Jesus is the gate for the sheepfold, through which the sheep enter and are saved. The distinction of Jesus as gate is significant and should not immediately be conflated with Jesus as Good Shepherd, which is stated explicitly later in this chapter. Here we see Jesus as the "Gate" with an accompanying image of the gatekeeper. The imagery is simple and ancient. Here there is not "heaven" but instead a place of safety and security from the world with its dangers and threats. Even this place of safety is not entirely secure, as there are some thieves and robbers who would climb the fence, not entering through the gate. Our only "protection" from such dangers is that we would not follow their voice.

This figure of speech should give us pause. Are we led astray by other voices in the culture—voices that might appeal to our preconceived ideologies or that would soothe us with simplistic and self-serving messages? Let us die to the other voices calling us away from gospel values. Let us know the gate through which we enter the sheepfold and not be called away by other voices.

✦ Jesus tells the Pharisees that his sheep will not follow a stranger, "because they do not recognize the voice of strangers." What spiritual practices help you attune your ears to the voice of the Good Shepherd?

Brief Silence

Prayer

Jesus, you promise to be the gate through which the sheep enter the fold. You are also the Good Shepherd whose voice is known by the sheep. Give us ears attentive to your voice so that we may follow you more closely in the midst of our daily activities, ever looking forward to entering the sheepfold at your direction. **Amen.**

In today's gospel Jesus proclaims himself "the way, the truth, and the life." May this water cleanse our hearts and minds, and draw us into even deeper union with Christ . . .

Prayer

Upright is your word, O God,
for you are the way, the truth, and the life.
All your works are trustworthy,
for you are the way, the truth, and the life.
Help us believe and follow you,
for you are the way, the truth, and the life.
Exult, you just, in the Lord. Alleluia!
Give thanks to the Lord. Alleluia! **Amen.**

Gospel   John 14:1-12

Jesus said to his disciples: "Do not let your hearts be troubled. You have faith in God; have faith also in me. In my Father's house there are many dwelling places. If there were not, would I have told you that I am going to prepare a place for you? And if I go and prepare a place for you, I will come back again and take you to myself, so that where I am you also may be. Where I am going you know the way." Thomas said to him, "Master, we do not know where you are going; how can we know the way?" Jesus said to him, "I am the way and the truth and the life. No one comes to the Father except through me. If you know me, then you will also know my Father. From now on you do know him and have seen him." Philip said to him, "Master, show us the Father, and that will be enough for us." Jesus said to him, "Have I been with you for so long a time and you still do not know me, Philip? Whoever has seen me has seen the Father. How can you say, 'Show us the Father'? Do you not believe that I am in the Father and the Father is in me? The words that I speak to you I do not speak on my own. The Father who dwells in me is doing his works. Believe me that I am in the Father and the Father is in me, or else, believe because of the works themselves. Amen, amen, I say to you, whoever believes in me will do the works that I do, and will do greater ones than these, because I am going to the Father."

Brief Silence

For Reflection

The opening words of today's gospel are addressed to the disciples, and we can imagine they are addressed to us as well: "Do not let your hearts be troubled. / You have faith in God; have faith also in me." These words were written to a community that did not have a history of trinitarian theology. Monotheism was in some ways challenged by Jesus' identity with the Father. We recall that Jesus was crucified for, among other things, blasphemy. The early Christians believed in Jesus. They also believed in God. Only centuries later, and after many disagreements and councils, trinitarian theology developed to a point where a common creed was held, in sophisticated language.

In our own lives, we might be patient with ourselves and others who have difficulty with grandiose trinitarian concepts and instead root our knowledge of Jesus in the Scriptures and personal experience, for that is akin to what the early Christians did. Ultimately, Christianity is about service in the name of Jesus rather than knowledge in the name of Jesus. Therefore, we have faith in Jesus, as we have faith in God, so that we might live to serve in his name.

✦ Jesus tells his disciples, "Do not let your hearts be troubled." Instead they are called to have faith in God and in him. Where have troubles entered into your life and how might you seek to turn them over to the Lord?

Brief Silence

Prayer

God, Father Almighty, you sent your Son into the world showing us the way of life. The same spirit that inspired the Scriptures, inspired his ministry, and it inspires us too. Awaken us to your spirit within us, so that we might imitate your Son, who came to serve rather than to be served. For you live and reign, one God, Father, Son, and Spirit, forever and ever. **Amen.**

In today's gospel Jesus tells us, "Whoever has my command-ments and observes them / is the one who loves me." May this water strengthen us in the life of discipleship as we seek to follow Jesus' path of love and mercy . . .

Prayer

If we love you, Lord, our God,
we will keep your commandments.
If we love you, Lord, our God,
we will never be orphaned.
May Christ the Lord be Lord in our hearts,
and we will keep your commandments.
Let all the earth cry out with joy. Alleluia!
Sing praise to the glory of God's name. Alleluia! **Amen.**

Gospel   **John 14:15-21**

Jesus said to his disciples: "If you love me, you will keep my commandments. And I will ask the Father, and he will give you another Advocate to be with you always, the Spirit of truth, whom the world cannot accept, because it neither sees nor knows him. But you know him, because he remains with you, and will be in you. I will not leave you orphans; I will come to you. In a little while the world will no longer see me, but you will see me, because I live and you will live. On that day you will realize that I am in my Father and you are in me and I in you. Whoever has my commandments and observes them is the one who loves me. And whoever loves me will be loved by my Father, and I will love him and reveal myself to him."

Brief Silence

For Reflection

As Christians we seek to follow the example of Christ, who poured himself out in love for his friends. Especially in the Gospel of John, we hear the word "love" often. For example, "God so loved the world that he sent his only son" (John 3:16), the simple and straightforward "God is love" (1 John 4:8), and of course the command to "love one another" (John 13:34; 15:12). The command seems so simple but it is very difficult to carry out. Here we have no list of duties or acts to perform, such as going to church or saying certain prayers. Instead, we have the profound command to love. Love knows no limits and there is not a point when we say "enough." Love sees the other as another self, so that the needs of the other are as important as our own. When modern communication has made the world a global village, the needs of our neighbors can seem overwhelming. Where do we stop? Yet, we are called to move beyond ourselves as Jesus did and to place our lives in service of the other, in imitation of him. Then we may merit the name "disciple," when we are known by our love.

✦ Jesus tells his disciples, "If you love me, you will keep my commandments." How would you summarize the commandments of the Lord? How do you strive to keep them in your daily life?

Brief Silence

Prayer

Jesus, you came into the world to show us the way of love, surpassing precepts of the law. May your example of love enliven us to show love to all those we meet. For it is our call as disciples to be ambassadors of your love in the world. May we as Christians be known by the love we have for all. In your name we pray. **Amen.**

Jesus commissions the apostles to go and "make disciples of all nations, / baptizing them in the name of the Father, / and of the Son, and of the Holy Spirit." May this water remind us of our own baptism and revitalize us to go forth and proclaim Christ to all we meet . . .

Prayer

Call us to go and make disciples, Lord,
for you are with us always;
to baptize them in your holy name,
for you are with us always;
and teach them to follow your way of love,
for you are with us always.
Sing praise to God, sing praise. Alleluia!
All people of God, sing hymns of praise. Alleluia! **Amen.**

Gospel   **Matt 28:16-20**

The eleven disciples went to Galilee, to the mountain to which Jesus had ordered them. When they saw him, they worshiped, but they doubted. Then Jesus approached and said to them, "All power in heaven and on earth has been given to me. Go, therefore, and make disciples of all nations, baptizing them in the name of the Father, and of the Son, and of the Holy Spirit, teaching them to observe all that I have commanded you. And behold, I am with you always, until the end of the age."

Brief Silence

For Reflection

The ascension is depicted so graphically in Acts that many of us read Matthew's story with Acts in the background. But the story of the ascension is not so much about Jesus magically rising into the air and being taken away by clouds, as it is about the last time he was seen by his disciples. Theologically, the more important aspect is what he says, not how he leaves. In the Gospel of Matthew, he commissions the disciples to evangelize, to tell the good news, making disciples on their way by baptizing. Indeed, in the Gospel of Matthew this message is so significant that Matthew does not even narrate an ascension!

And despite this last appearance, Jesus promises that he is with them. Earlier in the gospel Jesus spoke about how judgment will be based on how we treat the one who hungers or the one who thirsts, for in each encounter we see Jesus. When we serve the poor, we serve Jesus. When we neglect the poor, we neglect Jesus. Jesus is present among us always in the poor and lowly of the world. That is his promise.

✦ How does your faith community carry on the great commission that Jesus gave the first apostles to "make disciples of all nations" through baptism and teaching?

Brief Silence

Prayer

Lord Jesus, you ascended into heaven to reign with God, giving us a promise of our future destiny. Give us the grace to do your work on earth, feeding the hungry and giving drink to those who thirst, so that we might one day be with you in heaven. We ask this in your holy name. **Amen.**

In today's gospel Jesus prays to the Father, asking that he might give eternal life to his disciples. In the waters of baptism, we have died with Christ and risen as a new creation. May these waters remind us of our baptismal joy and bring us to fuller life in Christ . . .

Prayer

As he prepared to die on the cross,
Jesus prayed for us.
Though the hour of his death had come,
Jesus prayed for us.
Teach us to pray with one accord,
as Jesus prayed for us.
The Lord is my light and my salvation. Alleluia!
The Lord is my life's refuge. Alleluia! **Amen.**

Gospel   John 17:1-11a

Jesus raised his eyes to heaven and said, "Father, the hour has come. Give glory to your son, so that your son may glorify you, just as you gave him authority over all people, so that your son may give eternal life to all you gave him. Now this is eternal life, that they should know you, the only true God, and the one whom you sent, Jesus Christ. I glorified you on earth by accomplishing the work that you gave me to do. Now glorify me, Father, with you, with the glory that I had with you before the world began.

"I revealed your name to those whom you gave me out of the world. They belonged to you, and you gave them to me, and they have kept your word. Now they know that everything you gave me is from you, because the words you gave to me I have given to them, and they accepted them and truly understood that I came

from you, and they have believed that you sent me. I pray for
them. I do not pray for the world but for the ones you have given
me, because they are yours, and everything of mine is yours and
everything of yours is mine, and I have been glorified in them.
And now I will no longer be in the world, but they are in the
world, while I am coming to you."

Brief Silence

For Reflection

On the night before he died, Jesus prays not only for the disciples in
his day and time, but for us today. His prayers for us strengthen us
as we live in the midst of the world. He is no longer in the world as
he once was, but we are. In the face of all we encounter in the world,
we have an advocate in Jesus, and another advocate in the Spirit.

Christian identity, rooted in Jesus' identity, means that we live
in the world but are not of the world. God so loved the world that
he gave his only son. But he called those who were his own in the
world. The son came for us; we have been chosen. When we feel
called by the allure of the world, let us recall that the world is only
a temporary home for us. A bright future awaits where love reigns
and glory is resplendent.

The knowledge that Jesus prayed for us should humble us and
cause us to emulate him who came to serve rather than be served.
With eyes of faith, let us see anew and reorient our lives.

✦ In the gospel Jesus prays, "I glorified you on earth / by accomplishing the work that you gave me to do." How does your
work give glory to God?

Brief Silence

Prayer

Jesus, Advocate and Son of God sent into the world for our salvation, you returned from whence you came, giving us another
Advocate, the Spirit. Make us aware of the presence of the Spirit,
calling to mind your teachings, and reminding us of our true
destiny to be with you forever. We ask this in your holy name.
Amen.

The Holy Spirit descends on the apostles like "tongues as of fire." May this water remind us of the waters of baptism, which gifted us with this same Spirit . . .

Prayer

Come, Spirit, come:
from your celestial home!
Come, Spirit, come:
the Source of all good!
Come, Spirit, come:
most blessed Light divine!
Fill the hearts of your faithful. Alleluia!
And kindle in them the fire of your love. Alleluia! **Amen.**

Gospel   John 20:19-23

On the evening of that first day of the week, when the doors were locked, where the disciples were, for fear of the Jews, Jesus came and stood in their midst and said to them, "Peace be with you." When he had said this, he showed them his hands and his side. The disciples rejoiced when they saw the Lord. Jesus said to them again, "Peace be with you. As the Father has sent me, so I send you." And when he had said this, he breathed on them and said to them, "Receive the Holy Spirit. Whose sins you forgive are forgiven them, and whose sins you retain are retained."

Brief Silence

For Reflection

How many of us would like to have been present during the ministry of Jesus, or even during that of the early Christians? What would it have been like to hear the words of Peter at Pentecost? What would it have been like to have seen the risen Jesus and to have heard him say, "Peace be with you" before handing on the Holy Spirit? Yet, for those of us in the twenty-first century, we experience that same Holy Spirit. When we were baptized, we were given the gift of the Spirit, and then we were sealed by that same Spirit in confirmation. The Holy Spirit lives in our parishes, families, friends, and relationships. Once we experience the dying and rising of Christ, we live in a newness of life accompanied and animated by the Holy Spirit.

After he rose from the dead, Jesus gave his Holy Spirit to be with us. In our daily lives, let us allow ourselves to be guided by the Spirit of Christ, whose disciples we are.

✦ In today's gospel, Jesus greets his disciples by offering them peace. How do you strive to bring Christ's peace to those you greet each day?

Brief Silence

Prayer

Jesus Christ, bearer of peace, and giver of the Spirit, you showered these gifts on your disciples at Pentecost. Give these same gifts to us your disciples today. So empowered, we will do your work on earth, bearing peace to all those we meet. In your name we pray. **Amen.**

Our gospel for today tells us that "God did not send his Son into the world to condemn the world, / but that the world might be saved through him." With faith in God's loving kindness, let us pause to ask for his mercy and healing . . .

Prayer

Out of so great a love, Father, you sent your Son to save us.
Through your Holy Spirit, unite us in love
that we may share in your eternal life.
Glory to the Father, the Son, and the Holy Spirit:
Glory and praise forever! **Amen.**

Gospel   John 3:16-18

God so loved the world that he gave his only Son, so that everyone who believes in him might not perish but might have eternal life. For God did not send his Son into the world to condemn the world, but that the world might be saved through him. Whoever believes in him will not be condemned, but whoever does not believe has already been condemned, because he has not believed in the name of the only Son of God.

Brief Silence

For Reflection

On this the feast of the Most Holy Trinity, we have one of the shortest gospel readings of the year, and this from the Gospel of John. The passage is only three verses and it is proclaimed at the Liturgy of the Eucharist often in less than a minute, no more than two. The opening line of this gospel reading will be familiar to many, as it may be used frequently to sum up Christian theology: "God so loved the world that he gave his only Son."

This pithy statement grounds God's action and motivation in love. God is not an angry parent waiting for wayward humanity to make inevitable mistakes, only so he can punish. No, "God is love" (1 John 4:8). It is this same love that reflects God's desire to give (not merely to send) his only Son. The Son of God is given as a gift to the world out of love. As followers of this same Son, we ought to be motivated by love as well. We freely give without counting the cost; and we give not merely from our excess, but we give our very selves. That is the mark of a Christian disciple.

✦ Our gospel today begins with one of the most well-known lines in Holy Scripture: "God so loved the world that he gave his only Son." What does this action tell us about the one we call Father?

Brief Silence

Prayer

God of love, light, and life, you sent your Son into the world because you so loved the world. With the gift of your Son, may we his disciples be instruments of this same love. May all of our encounters increase love in the world and in so doing, spread peace and joy. Then, we will be known truly as disciples. **Amen.**

On this feast of Corpus Christi, Jesus tells us, "I am the living bread that came down from heaven." As we prepare to meet the risen Lord in the word of God and in the Eucharist, let us recall our sins and ask for God's pardon and mercy . . .

Prayer

We praise you, Lord, for you have blessed us
with a shelter strong and peaceful lives.
Unite us in the one cup and the one bread we share in Christ.
Blood is poured and flesh is broken.
From our hearts let praises sing. **Amen.**

Gospel   John 6:51-58

Jesus said to the Jewish crowds: "I am the living bread that came down from heaven; whoever eats this bread will live forever; and the bread that I will give is my flesh for the life of the world."

The Jews quarreled among themselves, saying, "How can this man give us his flesh to eat?" Jesus said to them, "Amen, amen, I say to you, unless you eat the flesh of the Son of Man and drink his blood, you do not have life within you. Whoever eats my flesh and drinks my blood has eternal life, and I will raise him on the last day. For my flesh is true food, and my blood is true drink. Whoever eats my flesh and drinks my blood remains in me and I in him. Just as the living Father sent me and I have life because of the Father, so also the one who feeds on me will have life because of me. This is the bread that came down from heaven. Unlike your ancestors who ate and still died, whoever eats this bread will live forever."

Brief Silence

For Reflection

On this feast of the Most Holy Body and Blood of Christ, also known as Corpus Christi (Latin for "Body of Christ"), the gospel reading is not from the Last Supper as we might expect. Instead, the reading is from part of the "bread of life discourse" of the Gospel of John. The eucharistic theology is up-front and paramount. Jesus proclaims that he is the living bread come down from heaven. He states clearly that this is true food and true drink. The imagery is so stark that many stumble over this teaching. Still Jesus maintains that those who consume this bread will live forever.

Later theologians build on this to say that it is precisely because Christians consume the Eucharist that we have the hope of eternal life. The Eucharist is the guarantor or the seed of eternal life that will come to fruition on the last day. Irenaeus, for example, says that when we receive the Eucharist, our bodies are no longer corruptible but have the hope of the resurrection to eternity (Irenaeus, *Against Heresies*, 4.18.5). Thus, the church gives us this feast day to reflect on the sacramental life by which we participate in the divine life.

✦ On the feast of Corpus Christi we revere the gift of the Eucharist in our lives. This past year, how has this gift of Christ's Body and Blood affected your life?

Brief Silence

Prayer

Lord Jesus, Bread of life come down from heaven, you make yourself known through the eucharist, the gift of bread and wine. May we be nourished by this gift often, and so receiving it become more like you, for we are your disciples. Your eucharist itself is our promise of eternal life, and for it we in turn say thank you. In gratitude we pray. **Amen.**

In today's gospel Jesus tells his disciples three times that they are not to fear. With abounding trust in the mercy of God, let us turn to him and ask for pardon and peace . . .

Prayer

O God, you have rescued the life of the poor
from the power of the wicked.
May we never be afraid to proclaim your Gospel.
Let the heavens and the earth praise God
who hears and answers those in need. **Amen.**

Gospel   Matt 10:26-33

Jesus said to the Twelve: "Fear no one. Nothing is concealed that will not be revealed, nor secret that will not be known. What I say to you in the darkness, speak in the light; what you hear whispered, proclaim on the housetops. And do not be afraid of those who kill the body but cannot kill the soul; rather, be afraid of the one who can destroy both soul and body in Gehenna. Are not two sparrows sold for a small coin? Yet not one of them falls to the ground without your Father's knowledge. Even all the hairs of your head are counted. So do not be afraid; you are worth more than many sparrows. Everyone who acknowledges me before others I will acknowledge before my heavenly Father. But whoever denies me before others, I will deny before my heavenly Father."

Brief Silence

For Reflection

In the reading we hear today, maybe it is fitting that Jesus says to his disciples three times some variation of "fear not" or "do not be afraid." The disciples (and that includes us) are to be fearless. The basis of this fearlessness is the Father, who knows all—even the most seemingly insignificant things that we do not know (e.g., the hairs on our head). The Father even knows each and every sparrow. We, each human being, is worth more than two sparrows (which themselves were worth only a small coin in antiquity). So the disciples can rest assured: they can be fearless in facing the world, as they are worth a great deal in the sight of God. With this assurance, with this fearlessness, the disciples are emboldened to acknowledge Jesus and preach him to the ends of the earth (Matt 28:19-20).

The danger is for those who know Jesus but choose not to acknowledge him before others. As far as they are concerned, Jesus will not acknowledge them before the Father.

✦ Jesus says to the twelve, "Even all the hairs on your head are counted." How have you experienced this abundant love of God in your life?

Brief Silence

Prayer

Jesus, you tell your disciples as you tell us to "fear not." With the gift of the spirit and the promise of our baptism we go forth into the world boldly, proclaiming you and doing acts of service and love. Inspire us in times of trepidation to live our call with firm conviction, fearing not, but secure in the knowledge that we are yours. In your name we pray. **Amen.**

In the gospel Jesus tells his apostles, "[W]hoever does not take up his cross / and follow after me is not worthy of me." For the times we have failed in the life of discipleship, let us ask for mercy and healing . . .

Prayer

Great is the reward you give, O God, to disciples who care for
 those in need.
Help us to give of our lives and take up our cross
that we may worthily follow your Son.
Forever I will sing the goodness of the Lord.
Through all generations my mouth shall sing God's praise. **Amen.**

Gospel   Matt 10:37-42

Jesus said to his apostles: "Whoever loves father or mother more than me is not worthy of me, and whoever loves son or daughter more than me is not worthy of me; and whoever does not take up his cross and follow after me is not worthy of me. Whoever finds his life will lose it, and whoever loses his life for my sake will find it. Whoever receives you receives me, and whoever receives me receives the one who sent me. Whoever receives a prophet because he is a prophet will receive a prophet's reward, and whoever receives a righteous man because he is a righteous man will receive a righteous man's reward. And whoever gives only a cup of cold water to one of these little ones to drink because the little one is a disciple—amen, I say to you, he will surely not lose his reward."

Brief Silence

For Reflection

The Christian life is marked by paradox, the greatest of which is the God-human Jesus. But many more paradoxes abound: death leads to life, to give is to receive, and emptying oneself is the means to fulfillment. The gospel reading today reflects some of these fundamental Christian paradoxes as well: "Whoever finds his life will lose it, and whoever loses his life for my sake will find it." This kind of teaching is fairly common among religious wisdom figures, and we shouldn't be surprised to hear it on the lips of Jesus.

Those worthy of Jesus are the ones who take up their cross and follow him. This does not mean to seek out suffering and place oneself in harm's way merely for the sake of it. Taking up one's cross refers to managing any and all of the difficulties and challenges that come with following Jesus. The image of the cross calls to mind violent and public execution at the hands of the state. It also foreshadows Jesus' own end on a cross. His followers should not shy away from such duties that flow naturally from being a Christian. As Jesus did, to gain life we must give it away. This is the ultimate paradox.

✦ Jesus tells the apostles, "[W]hoever does not take up his cross / and follow after me is not worthy of me." What does the cross look like that you are called to carry?

Brief Silence

Prayer

Lord Jesus, you took up your cross and in so doing set an example for us. When the burdens and cares we all experience seem too much, give us the grace to walk in your footsteps. May your resoluteness in the face of danger and hostility, give us strength to face the challenges before us. In your name we pray. **Amen.**

The truths of the kingdom of God are revealed to the humble. Let us turn to the Lord and ask for him to strip away the pride and vanity that clouds our vision so that we might draw closer to him . . .

Prayer

Blessed are you, Father, Lord of heaven and earth;
you have revealed to little ones the mysteries of the kingdom.
Bind us to your humble, gentle yoke.
The Lord lifts up all who are falling
and raises up all who are bowed down. **Amen.**

Gospel
Matt 11:25-30

At that time Jesus exclaimed: "I give praise to you, Father, Lord of heaven and earth, for although you have hidden these things from the wise and the learned you have revealed them to little ones. Yes, Father, such has been your gracious will. All things have been handed over to me by my Father. No one knows the Son except the Father, and no one knows the Father except the Son and anyone to whom the Son wishes to reveal him.

"Come to me, all you who labor and are burdened, and I will give you rest. Take my yoke upon you and learn from me, for I am meek and humble of heart; and you will find rest for yourselves. For my yoke is easy, and my burden light."

Brief Silence

For Reflection

The relationship between the Father and Son is intimate and dynamic. Jesus beckons the disciples into this relationship with the invitation "come to me." The term "yoke" that follows would have conjured up the image of Mosaic Law. Of course, a yoke is a type of wooden harness, bar, or frame used to keep oxen (or cattle) driving in the same direction, at the urging of a master. Wisdom is sometimes referred to as a yoke (Sirach 51:26), as is the law, but not in a negative way. In the New Testament (not only in Matthew but elsewhere), Jesus' ways are also referred to as a yoke.

Jesus tells his disciples that he himself is the yoke, meek and humble of heart. The rest he promises comes from emulating his ways, his attitudes, his dispositions, and his general way of being in the world. The disciple is yoked to Jesus, and the disciple finds this to be a lightness in his or her way of being. The yoke is not burdening or overbearing.

When we are followers of Jesus, when we imbibe his attitudes, our lives will not be burdened but filled with joy or, as Pope Francis might refer to it, the joy of the gospel.

✦ How have you experienced the "yoke" of Jesus to be "easy" and his burden light? In other words, how do you experience the "joy of the gospel"?

Brief Silence

Prayer

Lord God Almighty, your Son acts as a helpmate for us, and even used the image of a yoke, to express that. May we find the yoke of your Son to be light as he promised. With his guidance and assistance may we always follow the right path, leading to your will. By so doing, we will be filled with the Spirit of joy. In the triune God we pray. **Amen.**

FIFTEENTH SUNDAY IN ORDINARY TIME

In today's gospel Jesus ends the parable of the sower by proclaiming, "Whoever has ears ought to hear." For the times we have ignored the word of God or closed our ears to the sound of his voice, let us ask for mercy and forgiveness . . .

Prayer

The seed is your word, O God, and Christ is the sower.
Open our eyes to see, our ears to hear, and our hearts to understand
your saving Word
that we may yield a fruitful harvest for you.
God has crowned the year with goodness.
Let us shout and sing for joy. **Amen.**

Gospel   Matt 13:1-9 (or Matt 13:1-23)

On that day, Jesus went out of the house and sat down by the sea. Such large crowds gathered around him that he got into a boat and sat down, and the whole crowd stood along the shore. And he spoke to them at length in parables, saying: "A sower went out to sow. And as he sowed, some seed fell on the path, and birds came and ate it up. Some fell on rocky ground, where it had little soil. It sprang up at once because the soil was not deep, and when the sun rose it was scorched, and it withered for lack of roots. Some seed fell among thorns, and the thorns grew up and choked it. But some seed fell on rich soil and produced fruit, a hundred or sixty or thirtyfold. Whoever has ears ought to hear."

Brief Silence

For Reflection

The parable of the sower is rooted in antiquity with the image of scattering seed on the ground, which would have preceded plowing. Today even gardeners often sow seed by plowing first, planting the seed, then covering the seed with soil. But that is not the way those in the ancient world performed the task. It's for this reason that many seeds may be eaten by the birds or may fall on rocky soil. Not all the seed that is scattered takes root and bears fruit. Indeed, if those in the ancient world planted seeds the way a modern gardener does, it's highly unlikely that Jesus would have used this same parable! Instead, we might have a parable about the care with which the sower sows seed. But such is not the world of antiquity. Fortunately for us (and for the early disciples), Jesus himself explained the parable of the sower. There is no need to discern the intended meaning. Those who read the longer gospel today have the advantage of that explanation. And Jesus ends this simple allegorical tale with an injunction: "Whoever has ears ought to hear." Today, we might pray for the grace to grow where we find ourselves and to produce as much fruit as possible.

✦ Looking back on your life through the lens of today's parable, have you experienced environments that have been like rocky ground, thorny ground, or rich soil?

Brief Silence

Prayer

Lord God, your Son taught us that you are the sower and we are the seed. Give us the grace to grow where we are cast, producing a bountiful harvest. Grant us your Spirit by which such growth can take place, for you live and reign forever, one God, Father, Son, and Spirit. **Amen.**

In today's gospel Jesus proposes many parables to describe the kingdom of God. As we prepare to greet the Lord in the Scriptures and the Eucharist, let us pause to ask forgiveness for the times we have failed to build up the kingdom in our words or in our actions . . .

Prayer

Father, there is no god besides you who have the care of all
for you show your might through your mercy.
May we be just, kind, and merciful like you.
Lord, you are good and forgiving,
abounding in kindness and fidelity. **Amen.**

Gospel   Matt 13:24-30 (or Matt 13:24-43)

Jesus proposed another parable to the crowds, saying: "The kingdom of heaven may be likened to a man who sowed good seed in his field. While everyone was asleep his enemy came and sowed weeds all through the wheat, and then went off. When the crop grew and bore fruit, the weeds appeared as well. The slaves of the householder came to him and said, 'Master, did you not sow good seed in your field? Where have the weeds come from?' He answered, 'An enemy has done this.' His slaves said to him, 'Do you want us to go and pull them up?' He replied, 'No, if you pull up the weeds you might uproot the wheat along with them. Let them grow together until harvest; then at harvest time I will say to the harvesters, "First collect the weeds and tie them in bundles for burning; but gather the wheat into my barn."'"

Brief Silence

For Reflection

The shorter gospel reading today is about the weeds and the wheat, whereas the longer reading includes other parables. The parable of the weeds and the wheat occurs only in Matthew. The good sower expects a harvest of wheat but is unaware that his enemy cast weeds into the field. The precise term for the weed is "darnel," which is a plant that looks like wheat. Darnel is sometimes called "false wheat." Rather than uproot the darnel, a process that would harm the wheat, both are allowed to grow together. In the end there will be a sorting, and the darnel is destined for the fire.

Such an apocalyptic image requires little imagination. This is hardly the sort of parable whose meaning is difficult to discern. Instead, we see clearly that the followers of Jesus, the "church" (Matthew is the only gospel to use that term), is a field of wheat and weeds, the good and the bad. The church does not (or should not) play God and determine who will be uprooted. Instead, uprooting is God's role and he will perform it . . . in the end.

✦ Of today's many parables, which one speaks to you the most about the mystery of the kingdom of God? What does it reveal?

Brief Silence

Prayer

Lord God, Father of all, your son reminds us that there are weeds within the wheat, challenges inherent in being members of the Church. Give us the grace and patience to grow in the midst of such challenges, knowing that in the end it is for you to judge. May we be found to have produced a rich harvest on that day, so that we may enjoy eternal life with you. We pray. **Amen.**

In the first reading King Solomon asks God to grant him "an understanding heart / to judge your people and to distinguish right from wrong." Let us turn to the giver of every good gift and ask for his pardon and mercy . . .

Prayer

You have given us everything that is good, O God.
Yet we desire and are distracted by things that will not last.
Teach us to seek only the treasure of serving you.
Your commands, Lord, are finer than gold,
more precious to me than silver. **Amen.**

Gospel   **Matt 13:44-52 (or Matt 13:44-46)**

Jesus said to his disciples: "The kingdom of heaven is like a treasure buried in a field, which a person finds and hides again, and out of joy goes and sells all that he has and buys that field. Again, the kingdom of heaven is like a merchant searching for fine pearls. When he finds a pearl of great price, he goes and sells all that he has and buys it. Again, the kingdom of heaven is like a net thrown into the sea, which collects fish of every kind. When it is full they haul it ashore and sit down to put what is good into buckets. What is bad they throw away. Thus it will be at the end of the age. The angels will go out and separate the wicked from the righteous and throw them into the fiery furnace, where there will be wailing and grinding of teeth.

"Do you understand all these things?" They answered, "Yes." And he replied, "Then every scribe who has been instructed in the kingdom of heaven is like the head of a household who brings from his storeroom both the new and the old."

Brief Silence

For Reflection

This particular gospel reading preserves parables not found anywhere else in the New Testament, for example, the treasure buried in the field, and the pearl of great price. Each parable makes a similar point with Jesus instructing his disciples that the kingdom of heaven is worth such a price. In other words, once one encounters the kingdom of heaven, a proper response is to reprioritize all else in favor of this. It is worth selling everything else to possess this one thing.

The longer gospel reading gives one more parable, but it has another point. Rather than reinforce the lesson of the first two parables, the third—the net cast into the sea which brings in a terrific catch—has another message. The net is returned with good fish, but also with things that are not so good. The latter is thrown away. This then becomes the image for the eschatological judgment, a topic that Matthew addresses quite often. At the judgment, some will be not merely cast aside or "thrown away," but the angels will throw the wicked into the "fiery furnace." Matthew is sure to tell us there will be a final, definitive judgment and an unfortunate end is possible based on the decisions we have made.

✦ Considering the parables of the precious pearl and the hidden treasure, what do you think Jesus wants us to know about the kingdom of God?

Brief Silence

Prayer

Lord Jesus, Great and Gifted Teacher, you tell us that the Kingdom is akin to a pearl of great price, or a treasure buried in the field. With this knowledge, may we align our choices to reflect this priority: the kingdom of heaven. May this be our desire above all else. In your name we pray. **Amen.**

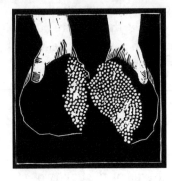

In a deserted place, Jesus feeds over five thousand people with five loaves and two fish. Trusting in the abundance of our Lord, let us turn to him and ask for mercy and healing . . .

Prayer

You feed us, Lord, not with bread alone but with your life-giving word.

Most of all you nourish us with the love of your Son, Jesus.

In his name, let us be food for others.

The hand of the Lord feeds us;

God answers all our needs. **Amen.**

Gospel   Matt 14:13-21

When Jesus heard of the death of John the Baptist, he withdrew in a boat to a deserted place by himself. The crowds heard of this and followed him on foot from their towns. When he disembarked and saw the vast crowd, his heart was moved with pity for them, and he cured their sick. When it was evening, the disciples approached him and said, "This is a deserted place and it is already late; dismiss the crowds so that they can go to the villages and buy food for themselves." Jesus said to them, "There is no need for them to go away; give them some food yourselves." But they said to him, "Five loaves and two fish are all we have here." Then he said, "Bring them here to me," and he ordered the crowds to sit down on the grass. Taking the five loaves and the two fish, and looking up to heaven, he said the blessing, broke the loaves, and gave them to the disciples, who in turn gave them to the crowds. They all ate and were satisfied, and they picked up the fragments left over—twelve wicker baskets full. Those who ate were about five thousand men, not counting women and children.

Brief Silence

For Reflection

Bread is such a simple but profound sign. It does not occur naturally, but requires human effort. Grain must be crushed to form flour. Flour is mixed with water or some other liquid to form dough, and the dough must be leavened with yeast to rise. Then the baking begins and we finally have a loaf of bread, sustenance that will fill us up and last. The human effort required to make bread is significant, and it involves time, all of which perhaps explains why so many of us simply buy bread today. Even so, there are not many things that taste better than a good loaf of homemade bread.

When we consider that Jesus multiplied the loaves so that all could eat, we recall that he acted as the prophet Elisha of old (2 Kgs 4:42-44). He also foreshadowed his own Last Supper and the eucharistic gift he would leave his followers. As a result, even today we take bread, bless it, break it, and give it. In so doing we celebrate and consume Jesus himself, who was broken for us and given to us. We are sustained on our earthly journey by the Eucharist.

✦ Jesus' miracles show us what life is like in the kingdom of God. From today's miracle of feeding the five thousand from five loaves and two fish, what message do you receive about the kingdom?

Brief Silence

Prayer

Jesus Christ, you come to us in the Eucharist so that we might be nourished on our earthly journey to you. Stir up in us a deep desire for your sacramental presence, and may we be fed spiritually upon receiving it, for you are the true bread come down from heaven. In your name we pray. **Amen.**

In today's gospel when Peter begins to sink, Jesus catches him and asks, "O you of little faith, why did you doubt?" For the times our own faith has faltered, let us ask for pardon and healing . . .

Prayer

You chose to make your presence known in the tiniest whispering sound.
When wind and quake, fire and storm threaten us,
command us, Lord, to come to you and wait for your saving word.
I will hear what God proclaims:
peace, salvation, kindness, truth. **Amen.**

Gospel   Matt 14:22-33

After he had fed the people, Jesus made the disciples get into a boat and precede him to the other side, while he dismissed the crowds. After doing so, he went up on the mountain by himself to pray. When it was evening he was there alone. Meanwhile the boat, already a few miles offshore, was being tossed about by the waves, for the wind was against it. During the fourth watch of the night, he came toward them walking on the sea. When the disciples saw him walking on the sea they were terrified. "It is a ghost," they said, and they cried out in fear. At once Jesus spoke to them, "Take courage, it is I; do not be afraid." Peter said to him in reply, "Lord, if it is you, command me to come to you on the water." He said, "Come." Peter got out of the boat and began to walk on the water toward Jesus. But when he saw how strong the wind was he became frightened; and, beginning to sink, he cried out, "Lord, save me!" Immediately Jesus stretched out his hand and caught Peter, and said to him, "O you of little faith, why did you doubt?" After they got into the boat, the wind died down. Those who were in the boat did him homage, saying, "Truly, you are the Son of God."

Brief Silence

For Reflection

We might wonder why Jesus commanded his disciples to set out by boat at dusk to meet him on the other side. It does not sound like a very wise or prudent request, and especially so after the storm arose. Nevertheless, the disciples follow the advice of their master. Rather than meet them on the other side, during the darkest part of the night, the disciples experience Jesus walking on the water in the midst of the wind and storm. Impetuous Peter seeks to walk on the water too, but he is unable to do so due to his lack of faith. In the end, the Lord calms the storm and joins the disciples in the boat.

When we experience turbulence and storms, we may be reassured that the Lord is near. When we call, he answers. He will join us and the storms will subside. Is it any wonder this story has been read for centuries as an allegory for the relationship between Christ and the church? The boat may protect us from the storm, but we still experience the effects of the storm. It is only Jesus himself who can calm the waters.

✦ In the gospel reading Jesus calls out to the frightened disciples, "Take courage, it is I, do not be afraid." When have you needed courage to follow Jesus in the life of faith?

Brief Silence

Prayer

Jesus Christ, you walked on the water and calmed the storm before your disciples. Calm the storms in our own lives. Increase our faith so that we might rest assured, knowing you are with us always. In your name we pray. **Amen.**

In today's gospel we hear Mary's words: "My soul proclaims the greatness of the Lord." We, too, have gathered to sing the Lord's praises. Let us pause to ask for his healing and mercy that we might worship him well . . .

Prayer

O God, in Mary you reveal your promise to all your people.
Array us with the splendor of her faithfulness
that we may enter your courts with gladness and joy.
My soul proclaims the greatness of the Lord;
my spirit rejoices in God my savior. **Amen.**

Gospel   Luke 1:39-56

Mary set out and traveled to the hill country in haste to a town of Judah, where she entered the house of Zechariah and greeted Elizabeth. When Elizabeth heard Mary's greeting, the infant leaped in her womb, and Elizabeth, filled with the Holy Spirit, cried out in a loud voice and said, "Blessed are you among women, and blessed is the fruit of your womb. And how does this happen to me, that the mother of my Lord should come to me? For at the moment the sound of your greeting reached my ears, the infant in my womb leaped for joy. Blessed are you who believed that what was spoken to you by the Lord would be fulfilled."

And Mary said: / "My soul proclaims the greatness of the Lord; / my spirit rejoices in God my Savior / for he has looked with favor upon his lowly servant. / From this day all generations will call me blessed: / the Almighty has done great things for me, / and holy is his Name. / He has mercy on those who fear him / in every generation. / He has shown the strength of his arm, / and has scattered the proud in their conceit. / He has cast down the mighty from their thrones, / and has lifted up the lowly. / He has filled the hungry with good things, / and the rich he has sent away empty. / He has come to the help of his servant Israel / for he has remembered his promise of mercy, / the promise he made to our fathers, / to Abraham and his children forever."

Mary remained with her about three months and then returned to her home.

Brief Silence

For Reflection

Marian doctrines can seem to be neverending sources of division with our Christian sisters and brothers. This is one reason why it is so important that the church gives us words from Mary in today's gospel. During the Mass, the Liturgy of the Word, we read from Scripture. And today we hear Mary.

When Mary spoke these words proclaimed today in the liturgy, Jesus had not even been born. She was a young woman who was motivated by justice. God was on her side and she foresaw a great reversal. She had a vision that certainly would have inspired and informed Jesus. How, then, did she react upon Jesus' death? We know she remained with the disciples up to and including Pentecost. Her faith never seems to have been shaken. She seems to have been prepared for the ultimate reversal from death to life during her entire life. Let us, too, live this profound notion of discipleship as Mary did.

✦ Where have you seen, or how have you participated in, gospel values of justice and peace overcoming worldly values of selfishness and pride?

Brief Silence

Prayer

Lord Jesus Christ, your mother Mary lived discipleship much as we strive to do so today. May we look to her and her example of gospel values in our own day and age. We ask this in your name for you live and reign with the Father and Spirit, one God, forever and ever. **Amen.**

As we prepare to meet the risen Lord in his Word and at the altar, let us pause to call to mind our sins so that we might ask the Lord for his mercy . . .

Prayer

Those the world rejects, Lord—the stranger, the foreigner,
the one who disrupts our daily routine—are first to receive
   your mercy.
Grant us their great faith in you.
O God, let all the nations praise you!
May all the peoples praise you, O God. **Amen.**

Gospel   Matt 15:21-28

At that time, Jesus withdrew to the region of Tyre and Sidon. And behold, a Canaanite woman of that district came and called out, "Have pity on me, Lord, Son of David! My daughter is tormented by a demon." But Jesus did not say a word in answer to her. Jesus' disciples came and asked him, "Send her away, for she keeps calling out after us." He said in reply, "I was sent only to the lost sheep of the house of Israel." But the woman came and did Jesus homage, saying, "Lord, help me." He said in reply, "It is not right to take the food of the children and throw it to the dogs." She said, "Please, Lord, for even the dogs eat the scraps that fall from the table of their masters." Then Jesus said to her in reply, "O woman, great is your faith! Let it be done for you as you wish." And the woman's daughter was healed from that hour.

Brief Silence

For Reflection

In today's gospel, a Canaanite woman comes up to Jesus and asks for his mercy, not for her but for her daughter. It was "easy" to look down on a Canaanite, as they were not considered part of God's chosen people. Jesus' behavior, like that of the disciples, can seem a bit shocking. Jesus initially refuses to acknowledge the woman, and the disciples seek to have her dismissed. Jesus finally does speak, only to say that he was "sent only to the lost sheep of the house of Israel." That is, he was not sent for a Canaanite, even if her daughter was suffering.

Even so, the woman persists. She does not back away. Jesus replies, effectively reiterating what he had said initially, though using a rather insulting term: "dogs." No matter, the woman continues, accepts the insulting metaphor, and says even dogs get the scraps. Finally, Jesus relents, and with a word the woman's daughter is healed. The woman persisted and she ultimately received what she sought, not something for herself but for her daughter.

After the resurrection, Jesus tells his disciples to go to all nations, teaching and baptizing (Matt 28:16-20). The gospel message is inclusive, ultimately welcoming all.

✦ The Canaanite woman is persistent in her request that Jesus heal her daughter. Where are you being called to persistence in prayer?

Brief Silence

Prayer

Lord Jesus, you heard the cry of the Canaanite woman for her daughter, and you ultimately granted her request. Hear our cries too for those we love. Be attentive to our pleas. In your mercy, hear our prayer. **Amen.**

In today's gospel, Jesus asks the disciples, "Who do you say that I am?" We claim Jesus as Lord and savior, and so let us turn to him seeking forgiveness for the times we have failed in the life of discipleship . . .

Prayer

You give your church authority, O God, not to rule by fear or might but to loosen the chains of death and to bind us all to your Son. Teach us to use our power wisely.

In the presence of the angels I will sing your praise;

I will worship at your holy temple. **Amen.**

Gospel   **Matt 16:13-20**

Jesus went into the region of Caesarea Philippi and he asked his disciples, "Who do people say that the Son of Man is?" They replied, "Some say John the Baptist, others Elijah, still others Jeremiah or one of the prophets." He said to them, "But who do you say that I am?" Simon Peter said in reply, "You are the Christ, the Son of the living God." Jesus said to him in reply, "Blessed are you, Simon son of Jonah. For flesh and blood has not revealed this to you, but my heavenly Father. And so I say to you, you are Peter, and upon this rock I will build my church, and the gates of the netherworld shall not prevail against it. I will give you the keys to the kingdom of heaven. Whatever you bind on earth shall be bound in heaven; and whatever you loose on earth shall be loosed in heaven." Then he strictly ordered his disciples to tell no one that he was the Christ.

Brief Silence

For Reflection

The story in today's gospel reading from Matthew is a favorite in Catholic-Protestant dialogue or even debates on the role of Peter and the development of the papacy. But the papacy is a long way from the setting of this particular story. Simon Bar-Jonah confesses Jesus as the Christ. He recognizes Jesus for who he is, and Jesus responds by saying this insight was given to him by the heavenly Father. Jesus then names him "Peter," a Greek term meaning "Rock" (in Aramaic the term is *Kephas*).

Jesus then says that on this "rock" (whether "rock" in this instance refers to the person of Simon Bar-Jonah or his confession of Jesus as Christ is debated) he will build his "church." The term "church" appears in the gospels only here and in Matthew 18:17. Historically, churches developed later, after the time of Jesus, so it seems anachronistic for Matthew to use the term during the historical ministry of Jesus when no other gospel does. It's partially for that reason that the phrase is thought to be a Matthean addition. Even so, Matthew is informing, or reminding, his audience that Peter was a spokesperson for the group, confessed Jesus as Christ, but even this was not due to his insight but from a gift of the Father.

✦ In today's gospel Peter answers Jesus' question, "Who do you say that I am?" by proclaiming, "You are the Christ, the Son of the living God." How do you announce who you believe Jesus to be through your words and actions?

Brief Silence

Prayer

Lord Jesus, your disciple Simon Bar-Jonah rightly confessed you as "Messiah." Give us the courage to confess you in our own day and age. So emboldened we will live more fully as your disciples, performing acts of service and love to those we meet, and so reflect our Christian identity. In you, the Christ, we pray. **Amen.**

In today's gospel Jesus calls us to deny ourselves, take up our crosses, and follow him. As we begin our celebration, let us turn to the Lord seeking healing and pardon for the times we have failed in the life of faith . . .

Prayer

Lord, our hearts desire to follow you, yet our thoughts keep
    counting the cost.
Captivate us with your mercy that we may conform our minds
    to Christ
to discern what is good, pleasing, and perfect.
I will bless you while I live;
with exultant lips my mouth shall praise you. **Amen.**

Gospel   **Matt 16:21-27**

Jesus began to show his disciples that he must go to Jerusalem and suffer greatly from the elders, the chief priests, and the scribes, and be killed and on the third day be raised. Then Peter took Jesus aside and began to rebuke him, "God forbid, Lord! No such thing shall ever happen to you." He turned and said to Peter, "Get behind me, Satan! You are an obstacle to me. You are thinking not as God does, but as human beings do."

Then Jesus said to his disciples, "Whoever wishes to come after me must deny himself, take up his cross, and follow me. For whoever wishes to save his life will lose it, but whoever loses his life for my sake will find it. What profit would there be for one to gain the whole world and forfeit his life? Or what can one give in exchange for his life? For the Son of Man will come with his angels in his Father's glory, and then he will repay all according to his conduct."

Brief Silence

For Reflection

The paradoxical sayings of Jesus are on full display today, following Peter's proclamation of him as Messiah. The paradoxes come to the fore because of Peter's misunderstanding of what it means to be the Messiah. Rather than victory and a glorious reign (which apparently is what Peter had in mind), Jesus rebukes him to say that his Messiahship will lead to his death. Only then will he be raised.

As the meaning of discipleship becomes more clear, we can wonder how Jesus had any remaining disciples! If the cost of discipleship is one's very life, perhaps it's better not to be a disciple? In the gospels it's clear that "would-be disciples" do in fact leave Jesus—they cease to follow him. But Peter and the others maintain their relationship with him, allowing it to go deeper, into a more full and complete understanding. By seeking to save one's life, it will be lost. By giving away one's life, it will be saved. To be the reigning, victorious Messiah means a life that ends in suffering and death. The paradoxical notions of Jesus' teaching are central to his wisdom.

✦ In the gospel Jesus says, "Whoever wishes to come after me must deny himself, / take up his cross, and follow me." What is the cross you have been given to bear?

Brief Silence

Prayer

Jesus, teacher of wisdom, give us the same wisdom that flows from you. Grant us the freedom to live the paradox of your teaching that death leads to life, and loss leads to gain. May we set aside worldly wisdom and embrace your teaching, for you live and reign as one God with the Father and Spirit, forever. **Amen.**

In his letter to the Romans, St. Paul pronounces, "[L]ove is the fulfillment of the law." For all the times our words and actions have been lacking in love, let us ask for pardon and mercy . . .

Prayer

How easy it is to complain about another, to gossip or slander, defame or despise.
Yet you have made us one family, Lord, bound together by love.
In Christ may we be reconciled.
Come, let us sing joyfully to the Lord;
let us acclaim the rock of our salvation. **Amen.**

Gospel   Matt 18:15-20

Jesus said to his disciples: "If your brother sins against you, go and tell him his fault between you and him alone. If he listens to you, you have won over your brother. If he does not listen, take one or two others along with you, so that 'every fact may be established on the testimony of two or three witnesses.' If he refuses to listen to them, tell the church. If he refuses to listen even to the church, then treat him as you would a Gentile or a tax collector. Amen, I say to you, whatever you bind on earth shall be bound in heaven, and whatever you loose on earth shall be loosed in heaven. Again, amen, I say to you, if two of you agree on earth about anything for which they are to pray, it shall be granted to them by my heavenly Father. For where two or three are gathered together in my name, there am I in the midst of them."

Brief Silence

For Reflection

Matthew's gospel today tells us how conflict resolution is to take place in a community of believers. Each disciple is empowered to correct any other when there is the occasion of sin. But this correction is to be done privately as a way to honor the reputation of the one being corrected and in light of the familial relationships that are the model for this community of disciples (cf. Matt 12:46-50).

Only if this one-on-one correction fails does the circle widen to include others, echoing Mosaic Law (Deut 19:15). If this too fails, the matter comes to the "church." Matthew envisions the church acting collectively and punishing a sinner by treating him "as you would a Gentile or a tax collector." That is to say, the sinner is cast outside the community. This advice might sound odd to us, but it reflects the Jewish roots of the Matthean community. Similar advice is found in Paul (1 Cor 5:1-8).

Thus, when we join a community of believers, it's not that we've found a community of perfection. Instead, we have a community of human beings—with faults, failings, and even sin. The church, and even individual believers, has an obligation to act when faced with sinful actions.

✦ In today's gospel Jesus outlines the way to resolve conflicts between disciples. What has been your own experience when facing conflicts within your parish community?

Brief Silence

Prayer

Lord God, conflict is unfortunately part of our life, but your Son taught us how to resolve such disagreements. May we be inspired by his teaching, reflecting and modeling his example, so that there might be peace rather than strife, joy rather than antagonism. In so doing we will be known as his disciples. In his name we pray. **Amen.**

In today's gospel Jesus tells us we are to forgive "not seven times, but seventy-seven times." For the times we have failed in mercy to those who have harmed us, let us ask the Lord for healing and pardon . . .

Prayer

Father, you are slow to anger and rich in compassion.
In your mercy, we ask you,
forgive us our sins as we forgive those who sin against us.
Bless the Lord, O my soul;
and all my being, bless God's holy name. **Amen.**

Gospel   **Matt 18:21-35**

Peter approached Jesus and asked him, "Lord, if my brother sins against me, how often must I forgive? As many as seven times?" Jesus answered, "I say to you, not seven times but seventy-seven times. That is why the kingdom of heaven may be likened to a king who decided to settle accounts with his servants. When he began the accounting, a debtor was brought before him who owed him a huge amount. Since he had no way of paying it back, his master ordered him to be sold, along with his wife, his children, and all his property, in payment of the debt. At that, the servant fell down, did him homage, and said, 'Be patient with me, and I will pay you back in full.' Moved with compassion the master of that servant let him go and forgave him the loan. When that servant had left, he found one of his fellow servants who owed him a much smaller amount. He seized him and started to choke him, demanding, 'Pay back what you owe.' Falling to his knees, his fellow servant begged him, 'Be patient with me, and I will pay you back.' But he refused. Instead, he had the fellow servant put in prison until he paid back the debt. Now when his fellow servants saw what had happened, they were deeply disturbed, and went to their master and reported the whole affair. His master summoned him and said to him, 'You wicked servant! I forgave you your entire debt because you begged me to. Should you not have had pity on your fellow servant, as I had pity on you?' Then in anger his master handed him over to the torturers until he should pay back the whole debt. So will my heavenly Father do to you, unless each of you forgives your brother from your heart."

Brief Silence

For Reflection

Today's simple but profound story of the unrepentant debtor is unique to Matthew. One who owed the king an inordinate sum has no chance of paying it off. He will never earn that much and therefore he is essentially placed in debtors' prison, after all his assets, his very person, and his family were sold for cash value. The king, hearing the pleas of mercy, relents and releases the man from his debts and from prison. The king was moved by pity.

Then, the same man finds one who is in debt to him for a small amount. But rather than be moved by pity as the king was and emulate the forgiveness he was shown, the man casts the poor debtor in prison. The king is infuriated at the aborted forgiveness. We who have been forgiven are to forgive others, otherwise we may face the same fate as the one handed over to torturers if we do not forgive "from the heart."

✦ What has helped you when you found it difficult to forgive others for the harm they had done?

Brief Silence

Prayer

Lord God, you have forgiven us much, more than we can ever repay. May we who have been forgiven extend that same forgiveness to those who have hurt us. May your generosity and mercy inspire us to emulate that same generosity and mercy, and by so doing, we will be extending your work on earth. This we pray in the name of your son. **Amen.**

In today's second reading we are urged to "conduct yourselves in a way worthy of the gospel of Christ." For the times we have failed to act in a Christlike manner, let us turn to the Lord and ask for forgiveness . . .

Prayer

You are gracious and compassionate to all who call you, Lord, generous to the least among us and faithful to all.

Help us rejoice in your merciful love.

Every day will I bless you,

and I will praise your name forever. **Amen.**

Gospel   **Matt 20:1-16a**

Jesus told his disciples this parable: "The kingdom of heaven is like a landowner who went out at dawn to hire laborers for his vineyard. After agreeing with them for the usual daily wage, he sent them into his vineyard. Going out about nine o'clock, the landowner saw others standing idle in the marketplace, and he said to them, 'You too go into my vineyard, and I will give you what is just.' So they went off. And he went out again around noon, and around three o'clock, and did likewise. Going out about five o'clock, the landowner found others standing around, and said to them, 'Why do you stand here idle all day?' They answered, 'Because no one has hired us.' He said to them, 'You too go into my vineyard.' When it was evening the owner of the vineyard said to his foreman, 'Summon the laborers and give them their pay, beginning with the last and ending with the first.' When those who had started about five o'clock came, each received the usual daily wage. So when the first came, they thought that they would receive more, but each of them also got the usual wage. And on receiving it they grumbled against the landowner, saying, 'These last ones worked only one hour, and you have made them equal to us, who bore the day's burden and the heat.' He said to one of them in reply, 'My friend, I am not cheating you. Did you not agree with me for the usual daily wage? Take what is yours and go. What if I wish to give this last one the same as you? Or am I not free to do as I wish with my own money? Are you envious because I am generous?' Thus, the last will be first, and the first will be last."

Brief Silence

For Reflection

Jesus was a master teacher. His parables inspired and they were remembered in part because they were simple stories that conveyed multiple layers of meaning. Not only was Jesus a master teacher, but we recall that he taught two thousand years ago! One challenge is that some of his stories are set deeply in the milieu of his context. The parable we read today is not in fact making statements about modern labor law or the role of unions or day laborers. Instead, landowners in Jesus' time had incredible power over workers and over their property. Perhaps because there were no labor unions, guest worker programs, or labor laws to protect workers, the landowner was able to act with impunity. This kind of power makes for an apt image of a powerful and unaccountable God!

So Jesus uses the character of the landowner in the parable to say that God gives each his or her due at the very least, and he is generous. It is not up to us to tell God how and in what way he is to be generous with his resources. God gives to each what he will, though not less than what he promised.

✦ How do you feel about God's justice as portrayed in the parable of the laborers in the vineyard?

Brief Silence

Prayer

Lord Jesus, you are the master teacher, informing us of the meaning of discipleship and what that entails. Give us your spirit of perseverance so that we might live worthy of our call. Your Father, our God, is generous and gives what he will. We are grateful for all these gifts, in your holy name. **Amen.**

In today's second reading, St. Paul urges us to "[d]o nothing out of selfishness or out of vainglory; / rather, humbly regard others as more important than yourselves." For the times we have placed our needs above the needs of others, let us ask for pardon and mercy . . .

Prayer

We grumble in our selfishness, Lord, and place ourselves above
    others.
But you call us to turn away from our sin
that we may turn in love to you and do your will.
Your ways, O Lord, make known to me;
teach me your paths. **Amen.**

Gospel   **Matt 21:28-32**

Jesus said to the chief priests and elders of the people: "What is your opinion? A man had two sons. He came to the first and said, 'Son, go out and work in the vineyard today.' He said in reply, 'I will not,' but afterwards changed his mind and went. The man came to the other son and gave the same order. He said in reply, 'Yes, sir,' but did not go. Which of the two did his father's will?" They answered, "The first." Jesus said to them, "Amen, I say to you, tax collectors and prostitutes are entering the kingdom of God before you. When John came to you in the way of righteousness, you did not believe him; but tax collectors and prostitutes did. Yet even when you saw that, you did not later change your minds and believe him."

Brief Silence

For Reflection

As with all of Jesus' parables, the meaning of the "two sons" parable today is polyvalent. We can understand it in numerous ways, and this is precisely why the device of "parable" is so effective as a teaching tool. One apparent meaning is the favorite Matthean theme of doing versus saying (cf. Matt 7:21-23; 12:50; 23:3-4). Matthew's contention throughout the gospel is that not everyone who says "Lord, Lord" will enter the kingdom of heaven, but only those who do the will of the Father, which is to act mercifully particularly to those in need.

It's unfortunate that throughout history and even into the present day, there are many adherents of religion (this is not limited to Jews or Christians) who will talk a good game, but their actions indicate something else. We have many phrases in English that speak to this: "Actions speak louder than words," "By their actions you shall know them," "I don't believe what you say. I believe what you do," or "People lie, actions don't." All of these maxims get at one of the fundamental meanings of this parable.

✦ Considering today's parable, which son are you more likely to be (the one who commits but doesn't follow through, or the one who refuses but in the end complies)?

Brief Silence

Prayer

Lord Jesus, you taught your disciples using parables, and you teach us using the same. Grant us the courage of our words, so that our actions reflect our intentions. Let our "yes" mean "yes" and "no" mean "no." By so doing we will be ever closer to living as your true disciples, for our actions on behalf of the needy will match our words of praise and thanksgiving for you. **Amen.**

As we prepare to meet the Lord in the Holy Scriptures and the bread and wine of the Eucharist, let us call to mind our sins and ask for God's pardon and peace . . .

Prayer

You have planted in our hearts, O God, the seed of your Word and have tended it with your merciful care.
May we be good stewards of your grace.
O Lord, God of hosts, restore us;
shine your face upon us, and we shall be saved. **Amen.**

Gospel   **Matt 21:33-43**

Jesus said to the chief priests and the elders of the people: "Hear another parable. There was a landowner who planted a vineyard, put a hedge around it, dug a wine press in it, and built a tower. Then he leased it to tenants and went on a journey. When vintage time drew near, he sent his servants to the tenants to obtain his produce. But the tenants seized the servants and one they beat, another they killed, and a third they stoned. Again he sent other servants, more numerous than the first ones, but they treated them in the same way. Finally, he sent his son to them, thinking, 'They will respect my son.' But when the tenants saw the son, they said to one another, 'This is the heir. Come, let us kill him and acquire his inheritance.' They seized him, threw him out of the vineyard, and killed him. What will the owner of the vineyard do to those tenants when he comes?" They answered him, "He will put those wretched men to a wretched death and lease his vineyard to other tenants who will give him the produce at the proper times." Jesus said to them, "Did you never read in the Scriptures: / *The stone that the builders rejected / has become the cornerstone; / by the Lord has this been done, / and it is wonderful in our eyes? /* Therefore, I say to you, the kingdom of God will be taken away from you and given to a people that will produce its fruit."

Brief Silence

For Reflection

The image of the vineyard in the Gospel reading today is rooted (so to speak) in Isaiah 7, which is the first reading this Sunday. Jesus was familiar with Scripture and often used images from the sacred text in his teachings.

Often this parable is read in a way that reflects relations and tensions between Christians and Jews of Matthew's time. It's clear from Matthew's telling (though today's gospel ends before we read this section) that the chief priests and Pharisees certainly had no misunderstanding—they saw themselves in this parable and did not take kindly to it. They tried to arrest Jesus. But in the story proclaimed today, we do not hear the reaction of the chief priests and Pharisees.

From the early Christians' point of view, the Jews had Jesus killed and the Father had effectively opened up the vineyard (the kingdom of God) to the nations (Gentiles). The church today is clear that this reading does not mean the Jewish people were rejected (e.g., Pontifical Biblical Commission, *The Jewish People and Their Sacred Scriptures in the Christian Bible* [2002], 71). This parable and others like it in the Gospel of Matthew must be read with care, especially in light of both historical and modern Jewish-Christian relations.

✦ In the gospel Jesus quotes the Scripture passage, "The stone that the builders rejected / has become the cornerstone." Can you think of an example in your life where this proved to be the case?

Brief Silence

Prayer

Lord God Almighty, you are the master of the vineyard in which we labor. Give us the grace to recognize the great gift we have been given. Inspired by gratitude we shall thank you all the days of our lives. In the name of your Son we pray. **Amen.**

In today's gospel parable the guests initially invited to a wedding feast refuse to come. For the times we have not answered the invitation of the Lord in our own lives, let us pause to ask for pardon and mercy . . .

Prayer

You have prepared a wedding banquet for your people, O God, where all that has been broken may be joined by your saving love. May we be ready to respond to your invitation.
I shall live in the house of the Lord
all the days of my life. **Amen.**

Gospel   Matt 22:1-10 (or Matt 22:1-14)

Jesus again in reply spoke to the chief priests and elders of the people in parables, saying, "The kingdom of heaven may be likened to a king who gave a wedding feast for his son. He dispatched his servants to summon the invited guests to the feast, but they refused to come. A second time he sent other servants, saying, 'Tell those invited: "Behold, I have prepared my banquet, my calves and fattened cattle are killed, and everything is ready; come to the feast."' Some ignored the invitation and went away, one to his farm, another to his business. The rest laid hold of his servants, mistreated them, and killed them. The king was enraged and sent his troops, destroyed those murderers, and burned their city. Then he said to his servants, 'The feast is ready, but those who were invited were not worthy to come. Go out, therefore, into the main roads and invite to the feast whomever you find.' The servants went out into the streets and gathered all they found, bad and good alike, and the hall was filled with guests."

Brief Silence

For Reflection

In a story filled with such violence as we have today, it might be easy to forget we are dealing with a merciful God! God calls a people to himself and desires that they come to him. The destruction of the city of Jerusalem with its temple was interpreted at the time by Christians as God's judgment on Judah. A violent world saw stories of violence. Though we may wish to minimize the violence, unfortunately it has been part of human history from the beginning and continues to this day.

It might be difficult to strip away the violent imagery and focus instead on the kernel underneath it all. Matthew's church has the wisdom and experience of decades since the death and resurrection of Jesus. It has learned that there are some in the church who do not belong, as indicated in several parables. Sadly, our modern experience reflects this too. Simply being in the church does not make one holy, God's chosen, or a paragon of virtue. There are weeds within the wheat. Only God has the authority to definitively and eternally expel such a person. The sobering reminder that "many are invited but few are chosen" should cause us to pause, reflect, and reexamine our lives.

✦ In today's parable, Jesus likens the kingdom of God to a wedding feast. In what ways do you think this might be an apt description of heaven?

Brief Silence

Prayer

Good and gracious God, giver of the great banquet, you call many to be with you. Make us worthy of this call, so that we may respond generously to this gift. When you look upon us may you see your Son, in whose name we pray. **Amen.**

In Jesus we find the words of everlasting life and the way of salvation. As we begin our celebration, let us pause to ask for our ears to be opened to hear and follow the word of God . . .

Prayer

As your chosen people, Lord, you have made us citizens of heaven.
Help us reveal that your reign is here now
by giving you the rightful praise that belongs only to you.
Sing to the Lord a new song;
sing to the Lord, all you lands. **Amen.**

Gospel   Matt 22:15-21

The Pharisees went off and plotted how they might entrap Jesus in speech. They sent their disciples to him, with the Herodians, saying, "Teacher, we know that you are a truthful man and that you teach the way of God in accordance with the truth. And you are not concerned with anyone's opinion, for you do not regard a person's status. Tell us, then, what is your opinion: Is it lawful to pay the census tax to Caesar or not?" Knowing their malice, Jesus said, "Why are you testing me, you hypocrites? Show me the coin that pays the census tax." Then they handed him the Roman coin. He said to them, "Whose image is this and whose inscription?" They replied, "Caesar's." At that he said to them, "Then repay to Caesar what belongs to Caesar and to God what belongs to God."

Brief Silence

For Reflection

In the modern, rather individualistic world in which we live, there is a temptation to believe that what we have, we have earned. My possessions are mine, a result of my own hard work or that of others, such as family. But today's gospel is a good reminder that all we have is from God. As such, we should not and cannot be hoarders of God's good gifts. Even money itself should not be thought of as ours.

Jesus calls us to an entirely new way of thinking. We return to be fed at the table of his word and at the table of his Eucharist so often because we need to be reminded of this way of thinking when we are so immersed in the world with its ways.

Any resources we have are truly not our own. Even what we acquired through our own labor and efforts cannot be taken with us when we pass on from this life. Let us die to the notion of possessions—what is mine versus yours—and let us instead engage in a lifestyle of discipleship, which shares what we have with the least among us.

✦ Jesus tells the Pharisees, "[R]epay to Caesar what belongs to Caesar / and to God what belongs to God." What do you think he means by this teaching?

Brief Silence

Prayer

Good God, giver of all that is life-sustaining, give to us your children a spirit of gratitude and humility for all we have. May we never claim "mine" when we see what is yours. And may we emulate your generosity with all the gifts you have given to us. For you are a generous giver in whose name we pray. **Amen.**

In today's gospel Jesus proclaims the greatest commandment is to love God and the second is to love our neighbor as ourselves. For the times we have failed in keeping these commands, let us ask the Lord for pardon . . .

Prayer

Teach us, Lord, to imitate your Son, that we may love you
with all our heart, all our soul, and all our mind,
and love our neighbor as ourselves.
I love you, O Lord, my strength,
my rock, my fortress, my deliverer. **Amen.**

Gospel   Matt 22:34-40

When the Pharisees heard that Jesus had silenced the Sadducees,
they gathered together, and one of them, a scholar of the law,
tested him by asking, "Teacher, which commandment in the law is
the greatest?" He said to him, "You shall love the Lord, your God,
with all your heart, with all your soul, and with all your mind.
This is the greatest and the first commandment. The second is
like it: You shall love your neighbor as yourself. The whole law
and the prophets depend on these two commandments."

Brief Silence

For Reflection

In Jesus' day—when over 600 particular laws made up the totality
of Mosaic Law, and a violation of one effectively meant a violation

of the totality—the question posed to Jesus is seen as reasonable. But we should keep in mind that though the question seems perfectly legitimate on its face, the scholar was asking Jesus in order to test him.

That test doesn't seem to bother Jesus, who responds by quoting Mosaic Law, first Deuteronomy 6:5 followed by Leviticus 19:18. It's quite likely that Jesus himself was the first to combine these two commandments. When we love God and love our neighbor, we are fulfilling the law. All of the law, the entirety of the more than 600 particular laws, are summed up in these two.

For us today, we might think of something similar if one were to ask which is the most important teaching in the catechism, or which is the most important precept of the church. The answer sidesteps all these questions by saying the most important law is twofold: Love God and love your neighbor. With these as our guiding light, all else comes into focus.

✦ Jesus tells us the greatest and first commandment is "You shall love the Lord, your God." How do you keep your life centered around this commandment?

Brief Silence

Prayer

Lord God Almighty, giver of the Law and sender of your Son, Jesus, we strive to do your will. May we be motivated by love of you and love of neighbor all the days of our lives. Then we will be living by the standards of Jesus, in whose name we pray. **Amen.**

On this feast day, let us pray with all the saints that we might be brought to holiness and cleansed from sin . . .

Prayer

With you, O God, we are never alone
for the saints walk with us.
May their example teach us what it means to be blessed.
Blessing and glory, wisdom and thanksgiving,
honor, power, and might be to our God forever and ever. **Amen.**

Gospel   Matt 5:1-12a

When Jesus saw the crowds, he went up the mountain, and after he had sat down, his disciples came to him. He began to teach them, saying: / "Blessed are the poor in spirit, / for theirs is the Kingdom of heaven. / Blessed are they who mourn, / for they will be comforted. / Blessed are the meek, / for they will inherit the land. / Blessed are they who hunger and thirst for righteousness, / for they will be satisfied. / Blessed are the merciful, / for they will be shown mercy. / Blessed are the clean of heart, / for they will see God. / Blessed are the peacemakers, / for they will be called children of God. / Blessed are they who are persecuted for the sake of righteousness, / for theirs is the Kingdom of heaven. / Blessed are you when they insult you and persecute you and utter every kind of evil against you falsely because of me. Rejoice and be glad, for your reward will be great in heaven."

Brief Silence

For Reflection

The popular book *My Life with the Saints*, by the Jesuit James Martin, is an introduction to certain saints told through memoir. Some of the most famous and well-recognized saints are there, including St. Peter, Mary, the mother of Jesus, St. Ignatius of Loyola (the founder of the Jesuits), even Joan of Arc, Mother Teresa, and more, as well as some of the lesser known saints. Most of the saints he discusses, as reflected in the sample selection above, and as has been true throughout Christian history, were celibates.

So it's critically important that we have the words of the Beatitudes in today's gospel to remind us of what holiness looks like. Nowhere in the Beatitudes is a word about celibacy or, frankly, about sexuality at all. There is certainly nothing about one's vocational state (priest, sister, etc.). Instead, we have attributes such as "poor in spirit," "meek," and "merciful." These are the hallmarks of sanctity. And they can be practiced by anybody, religious or lay, Catholic or Protestant, even Christian or non-Christian. We recall that the Gospel of Matthew is much more about actions than words. And those actions have to do with mercy rather than celibacy.

✦ How do you strive to embrace the Beatitudes in your life of faith?

Brief Silence

Prayer

Lord Jesus, you taught your disciples the beatitudes which are in many ways a portrait of your very self, and a model for how to live as your disciples. When our lives are facing challenges and burdens, let us call to mind these markers of Christian identity. In so doing we will be reminded of you, and our own call to live in the world. In humility we pray. **Amen.**

Today's first reading tells us, "[T]he souls of the just are in the hand of God." Let us turn to the Lord and ask for pardon and healing that we may be counted among the just . . .

Prayer

You are God of the living, O Lord,
for in Christ, all the dead shall rise again.
May we who remember our beloved dead
join them in praise this day around your holy altar.
I believe that I shall see
the good things of the Lord in the land of the living. **Amen.**

Gospel   John 6:37-40 (see p. 133 for other gospel options)

Jesus said to the crowds: "Everything that the Father gives me will come to me, and I will not reject anyone who comes to me, because I came down from heaven not to do my own will but the will of the one who sent me. And this is the will of the one who sent me, that I should not lose anything of what he gave me, but that I should raise it on the last day. For this is the will of my Father, that everyone who sees the Son and believes in him may have eternal life, and I shall raise him up on the last day."

Brief Silence

For Reflection

It is significant that the church gives us this day, as it connects us with our ancestors in faith, such as deceased grandparents, great-grandparents, uncles, aunts, and extended family. We recall that together we form a "cloud of witnesses" (Heb 12:1) whose faith has been handed from one generation to the next. As St. Paul says, "So we preach, and so you believed" (1 Cor 15:11). Now in our present day, so many of us share the faith with others, who will in turn pass it down to others. It's hardly likely that we ourselves will be recognized by the church as a capital "S" saint, but due to our identity as disciples of Christ, one day we, too, may be remembered on this day fifty, or one hundred, or more years from now. We think not merely of ourselves but of generations to come.

The gospel passage the church uses to commemorate this feast is from John, with its universal character of salvation. In sum, God desires all to be saved. Then we shall be one family united in Christ. All those who have come before us, and all those yet to come, will be together.

✦ On All Souls' Day, who are the family or friends that have died who you celebrate and remember on this day?

Brief Silence

Prayer

Lord Jesus Christ, through the centuries you have gathered a "cloud of witnesses" to testify to you and your goodness. May we call to mind our own ancestors in faith, who taught us about you and gave us an example of Christian discipleship. May we too pass on this faith and in the distant future be numbered among the same "cloud of witnesses." Confident of your love for us we pray. **Amen.**

Other gospel options for November 2:

Matthew 5:1-12a / Matthew 11:25-30 / Matthew 25:31-46 / Luke 7:11-17 / Luke 23:44-46, 50, 52-53; 24:1-6a / Luke 24:13-16, 28-35 / John 5:24-29 / John 6:51-58 / John 11:17-27 / John 11:32-45 / John 14:1-6

In today's gospel, Jesus calls us to "stay awake" for we do not know "the day nor the hour" of his return. Let us pause to ask forgiveness for the times we have failed to be persistent in faith . . .

Prayer

Those who keep watch for you, O God, will never be disappointed. Focus our gaze that we may be awake and ready to see you where others fail to recognize your presence.
Thus will I bless you while I live;
my lips will call upon your name. **Amen.**

Gospel   **Matt 25:1-13**

Jesus told his disciples this parable: "The kingdom of heaven will be like ten virgins who took their lamps and went out to meet the bridegroom. Five of them were foolish and five were wise. The foolish ones, when taking their lamps, brought no oil with them, but the wise brought flasks of oil with their lamps. Since the bridegroom was long delayed, they all became drowsy and fell asleep. At midnight, there was a cry, 'Behold, the bridegroom! Come out to meet him!' Then all those virgins got up and trimmed their lamps. The foolish ones said to the wise, 'Give us some of your oil, for our lamps are going out.' But the wise ones replied, 'No, for there may not be enough for us and you. Go instead to the merchants and buy some for yourselves.' While they went off to buy it, the bridegroom came and those who were ready went into the wedding feast with him. Then the door was locked. Afterwards the other virgins came and said, 'Lord, Lord, open the door for us!' But he said in reply, 'Amen, I say to you, I do not know you.' Therefore, stay awake, for you know neither the day nor the hour."

Brief Silence

For Reflection

The parable Jesus tells in today's gospel may seem at first glance to be un-Christian. Why wouldn't the five who have oil share theirs with the five who do not have oil? But that's the wrong question. A better question would be, why weren't the five who have no extra oil prepared? They knew enough to bring their lamps, but they did not bring reserve flasks of oil. They had not anticipated that they would need more oil than what their lamp could hold. Rather than share, leading to a situation where nobody would have enough oil, the "wise" ones told the "foolish" to go get their own oil. And when they were gone, doing just that, the groom appeared, the guests entered, and the doors were locked. When the "foolish" ones returned, the master said he did not know them and they were not allowed in. Their cry of "Lord, Lord" calls to mind other passages in this gospel where people cry "Lord, Lord," only to hear the master reply that he does not know them (7:21-23; 25:31-46).

This is the same gospel that gives us the parable of the weeds and the wheat growing together. Matthew seems to be aware that the church is a mixed bag of the wise and the foolish.

✦ In today's parable the bridesmaids need oil so that their lamps might burn brightly at the arrival of the bridegroom. What is the oil that keeps your lamp of faith burning?

Brief Silence

Prayer

Lord God, you sent your Son into the world to teach us your ways. May we be attentive to his word, bearing oil in our lamps of faith our whole lives long. Let us not grow weary or lose heart, for we await your coming, our promise of eternal life and hope. In patient fortitude we pray. **Amen.**

Today's parable of the talents encourages us to use our gifts for the good of others. For the times we have not done this, let us ask for mercy and forgiveness . . .

Prayer

You have blessed us, Lord, with the desire to serve you.
May we use the gifts you entrust to us for the glory of your name,
for our good and the good of all your holy church.
Blessed are those who fear the Lord,
who walk in God's ways. **Amen.**

Gospel   Matt 25:14-30 (or Matt 25:14-15, 19-21)

Jesus told his disciples this parable: "A man going on a journey called in his servants and entrusted his possessions to them. To one he gave five talents; to another, two; to a third, one—to each according to his ability. Then he went away. Immediately the one who received five talents went and traded with them, and made another five. Likewise, the one who received two made another two. But the man who received one went off and dug a hole in the ground and buried his master's money.

"After a long time the master of those servants came back and settled accounts with them. The one who had received five talents came forward bringing the additional five. He said, 'Master, you gave me five talents. See, I have made five more.' His master said to him, 'Well done, my good and faithful servant. Since you were faithful in small matters, I will give you great responsibilities. Come, share your master's joy.' Then the one who had received two talents also came forward and said, 'Master, you gave me two talents. See, I have made two more.' His master said to him, 'Well done, my good and faithful servant. Since you were faithful in small matters, I will give you great responsibilities. Come, share your master's joy.' Then the one who had received the one talent came forward and said, 'Master, I knew you were a demanding person, harvesting where you did not plant and gathering where you did not scatter; so out of fear I went off and buried your talent in the ground. Here it is back.' His master said to him in reply, 'You wicked, lazy servant! So you knew that I harvest where I did not plant and gather where I did not scatter? Should you not then have put my money in the bank so that I could have got it back with interest on my return? Now then! Take the talent from him and give it to the one with ten. For to everyone who has, more will be given and he will grow rich; but from the one who has not, even what he has will be taken away. And throw this useless servant into the darkness outside, where there will be wailing and grinding of teeth.'"

Brief Silence

For Reflection
Jesus concludes the parable with some folk wisdom, reflecting common attitudes of the day (and even today), with a phrase akin to "the rich get richer and the poor get poorer." It would be a mistake to read this parable as somehow endorsing a political and economic system whereby the wealthy receive a majority of benefits while the poor suffer. Instead, that economic condition, which characterized the time of Jesus (and perhaps even our own!), becomes the folk wisdom reinforced by the parable.

The lesson from the parable has to do with the intervening time between the resurrection and the coming of Christ. How will the disciples (the servants) invest their own talents in service of the master? One must risk oneself to earn a reward. The investment of talent, skills, and gifts will generate returns. The miserable disciple who makes no personal investment, but instead uses the time prior to the coming of the Lord merely to loaf around, will be punished. He is hardly worthy of the name servant (disciple). Interestingly, the reward for the first two is the same, "Come, share your master's joy." But the third is exiled.

◆ What is one gift or talent that you have received from the hand of God and are using to serve God's people?

Brief Silence

Prayer

Lord Jesus, you rose to new life, ascended to heaven, and will return on the last day. Give us the patience to await your coming without losing hope. May we be inspired by your teaching and by your Eucharist so that we will be ready on that day to share our master's joy. In eternal hope we pray. **Amen.**

OUR LORD JESUS CHRIST, KING OF THE UNIVERSE

In today's gospel Jesus tells us that we will be judged on how we have treated others. For the times we have failed to provide and care for the poor and the vulnerable, let us ask for forgiveness . . .

Prayer

At the end of our days, Lord, you will ask not what we have
    accomplished
but whom we have loved and served.
May we be among those welcomed into your kingdom.
Only goodness and kindness follow me
all the days of my life. **Amen.**

Gospel   Matt 25:31-46

Jesus said to his disciples: "When the Son of Man comes in his glory, and all the angels with him, he will sit upon his glorious throne, and all the nations will be assembled before him. And he will separate them one from another, as a shepherd separates the sheep from the goats. He will place the sheep on his right and the goats on his left. Then the king will say to those on his right, 'Come, you who are blessed by my Father. Inherit the kingdom prepared for you from the foundation of the world. For I was hungry and you gave me food, I was thirsty and you gave me drink, a stranger and you welcomed me, naked and you clothed me, ill and you cared for me, in prison and you visited me.' Then the righteous will answer him and say, 'Lord, when did we see you hungry and feed you, or thirsty and give you drink? When did we see you a stranger and welcome you, or naked and clothe you? When did we see you ill or in prison, and visit you?' And the king will say to them in reply, 'Amen, I say to you, whatever you did for one of the least brothers of mine, you did for me.' Then he will say to those on his left, 'Depart from me, you accursed, into the eternal fire prepared for the devil and his angels. For I was hungry and you gave me no food, I was thirsty and you gave me no drink, a stranger and you gave me no welcome, naked and you gave me no clothing, ill and in prison, and you did not care for me.' Then they will answer and say, 'Lord, when did we see you hungry or thirsty or a stranger or naked or ill or in prison, and not minister to your needs?' He will answer them, 'Amen, I say to you, what you did not do for one of these least ones, you did not do for me.' And these will go off to eternal punishment, but the righteous to eternal life."

Brief Silence

For Reflection

In the gospel story, we are two days from Passover when Jesus will be handed over to be crucified (26:1-2). This teaching about how we will be judged is the crescendo of Jesus' message.

Jesus' promise to be with us always is fulfilled in that he is present in the hungry, thirsty, naked, ill, imprisoned, and in the stranger. Though some who claim to know Jesus are surprised that they did not see him in the face of the poor, this is to their own perdition. Even more, those who did not or do not know Jesus receive their heavenly reward precisely because they did the will of God; they fed the hungry and in so doing they were feeding Jesus. They gave drink to the thirsty and in so doing they were giving drink to Jesus. Jesus does not say that it is as though he is present in these people. No, he is them: "I was hungry and you gave me no food." "What you did not do for one of these least ones, you did not do for me." Again, Jesus identifies with the poor and the lowly, for he is them.

✦ How would you like to incorporate the corporal works of mercy into your life in the coming year?

Brief Silence

OUR LORD JESUS CHRIST, KING OF THE UNIVERSE

Prayer

Lord Jesus you promised to be with your disciples always. Today we see you as you promised, in the most needy of the world. By our service we know we are serving you. By our feeding the hungry we know we are feeding you. And by our giving drink to the thirsty we know we are giving drink to you. Nourished by your presence in the Eucharist we nourish you present in the needy. In gratitude we pray. **Amen.**